'The Big rhino cow staggered, blindly, through the moonlight bush, head down and the big log followed behind her jerking and catching and dragging the wire tighter into her neck, cutting deep screwing up her windpipe—as it was supposed to do—and the hyenas followed. She was dragging her hind foot, it buckled with the wire tight round the bone because all the muscles were severed, she lurched and then dragged the foot forward again, then buckled again. The calf stumbled after her and the hyenas waited.'

She had been caught in a ground snare, just one of the inhuman poaching methods that man uses to entrap the rhino and steal its horn. The snare doesn't kill, at least not at first, it maims and wounds and the terrified animal thrashes wildly at the wire, which sometimes snaps and then the agonized rhino lunges through the jungle leaving a bloody trail for the poacher or the hyenas to follow. *Operation Rhino* is the story of the battle to save the rhino in Rhodesia—a battle against the rugged terrain, the hostile rhinos and man ...

Also by John Gordon Davis

HOLD MY HAND I'M DYING
CAPE OF STORMS

and published by Corgi Books

John Gordon Davis

Operation Rhino

CORGI BOOKS
A DIVISION OF TRANSWORLD PUBLISHERS LTD
A NATIONAL GENERAL COMPANY

OPERATION RHINO

A CORGI BOOK 0 552 09331 9

Originally published in Great Britain
by Michael Joseph Ltd.

PRINTING HISTORY
Michael Joseph edition published 1972
Corgi edition published 1973

Corgi Books are published by Transworld
Publishers Ltd.,
Cavendish House, 57–59 Uxbridge Road,
Ealing, London, W.5.
Made and printed in Great Britain by
Cox & Wyman Ltd.,
London, Reading and Fakenham

**NOTE: The Australian price appearing on the
back cover is the recommended retail price.**

To
Clare Kelly Edwards

For all their advice and assistance in the gathering and prep-
aration of material for this book, I am deeply indebted to
Messrs. J. C. Tebbit, Ronald Thompson, Paul Coetsee,
Norman Payn, Richard Peek, Nevin Lees-May, Graham Hall
and John Osborne, all officers of the Department of National
Parks and Wildlife Management, Rhodesia Government.

In particular I am indebted to the Hon. Phillip Van Heerden,
Minister of Lands, for permitting me to accompany the
Operation Rhino expedition.

List of Illustrations

19. A beast is being goaded with sacks to charge out of its pen.
20. The same beast charges through the gap at the sack.
21. A beast is being heaved on to the sleigh.
22. A cow has been darted, and has fallen, and now her calf has also been darted. Photograph by Thompson.
23. This drugged beast, whilst still hobbled, has revived unexpectedly in the stockade.
24. The same beast has collapsed again, Thompson and Peek hang on.
25. Coetsee and Thompson are trying to catch a calf with ropes to avoid darting it. Photograph by Rhodesia Information Department.
26. A drugged beast staggers up before its legs have been roped. Photograph by Rhodesia Information Department.
27. A beast standing in the stockade, photographed through the gaps in the poles.
28. Coetsee tests the wind with an ash-bag.
29. A beast revives suddenly in the stockade; Coetsee leaps for safety.
30. A beast being released at Gona-re-Zhou.

PREFACE

THERE is a book called the *Red Data Book* which very few people know about. Published by the International Union for conservation of Nature and Natural Resources, in Switzerland, it lists the species of creatures in danger of extinction and the reasons therefor. There are presently one thousand types of vertebrate animals in this danger. Since Christ, the extinction rate has averaged one species every twenty years. Nowadays the rate is one species of mammal per year. And once they are gone, they are gone.

The Naked Ape is the reason. Man has abused, plundered, burnt, overpopulated, polluted. He cleaned out Europe long ago. Then he started colonizing. He hunted for game, kill kill kill, and introduced firearms to primitive men. He exploited and cut back the forests, stopped the internecine tribal wars and introduced modern medicine, death control but no birth control, and the human population explosion began, and the rape of the earth.

In Africa this rape, the impact of all these factors on the unfortunate wildlife has been devastating, very bloody and very cruel. One of the killers has been, and still is, the Tsetse Fly Control, the systematic killing, in certain areas, of game which host the tsetse fly, the purveyor of the dreaded, fatal sleeping sickness to man and domestic animals. But the biggest all-time killer has been the imposition of law and order and white man's medicine on primitive people who practise polygamy, who count their wealth in wives and cattle and daughters whom they sell as wives for cattle. This has resulted in massive population increase and massive encroachment upon the wildlife's natural habitat by people for whom the word for game is *nyama*, the same as the word for 'meat'.

The hunters are not only after meat, however. Even game rangers feel only moderately about the individual who of necessity or instinct hunts an animal with spear or bow and arrow or firearm to fill his family's belly. A scourge though such hunters are in modern Africa, because of the great increase in numbers doing it, they are only part of it. The real villains, the real bad bastards, are the professional poachers.

To them the meat is often only a by-product, often only waste matter to be left to rot under the African sun. They are really after the hides, horns, tusks, for sale to the middlemen, who sell them to the exporters down on the coast, who ship them round the world for trophies, mats, handbags, shoes, coats, suitcases, umbrella stands, necklaces, bangles, billiard balls, piano keys, ornaments, medicines, aphrodisiacs. Their best hunting grounds are the game reserves, which are by definition vast, remote, and difficult to police. They are the wholesale bastards, the dealers in the long, slow, crippling, thirst-crazed, death by the snares and the pits and the poison and the festering gun shot wounds. It is very big, bad business indeed.

The rhinoceros is listed in the *Red Data Book*. The beast has been hunted mercilessly for its horn. The horn is thought to be an aphrodisiac. It is powdered and taken like snuff, or carved into a goblet from which milk is drunk, and the snuff or the milk is reputed to be a much more powerful sexual stimulant than Spanish Fly or Cantharides Beetle. It does not work. Maybe the myth started because of the phallic shape of the horn. Anyway it started a long time ago. For two thousand years men have been paying a lot of money for a little bit of rhino horn. For two thousand years the rhinoceros has been hunted down down down. They hunted out the little Javan Rhinoceros and now there are two dozen or so left in the whole wide world; they hunted out the small Sumatran Rhino and now there are maybe two hundred left; they hunted the Great Indian Rhino down down down. And they came to Africa and hunted out the big wild White Rhino, almost clean out of North Africa and Central Africa and the whole of southern Africa; and they hunted down the Black Rhino, kill kill kill, snares and pits and arrows and muzzle-loaders and high-powered rifles. And all for the horn, which doesn't work anyway.

A number of operations have been mounted by different bodies and governments, with varying degrees of success, to translocate rhinos from areas where they are being poached, to safer reserves. A small nucleus survived in Natal, South Africa, which were given maximum protection in a sanctuary area and they now flourish there.

The Great Indian Rhino is increasing satisfactorily in numbers under the strict protection of the Indian and Nepalese governments, and there are now about seven hundred. The Sumatran Rhinos are scattered over half a dozen South-East Asian countries in small pockets inimical to breeding: an attempt at translocation for breeding purposes ended disastrously with two shot dead in self-defence and one female in a zoo. In 1970 the Rhodesian Government mounted a large operation to capture Black Rhino in remote pockets where their existence was badly threatened by poachers, to translocate them to the other end of the country, to the vast Gona-re-Zhou game reserve.

Black Rhinos are the most dangerous of the highly dangerous family. They are over five feet tall at the shoulder, some as tall as an average man. They are up to ten feet long, weight over two thousand pounds, they can run at twenty-five miles an hour, and can turn about, at that speed, in twenty feet. They are armed with a sharp vicious horn sometimes over two feet long, they have acute smell and hearing senses, they are highly irascible and given to Herculean murderous charges at their well-intentioned captors. Capturing them alive in their rugged habitat, and then moving the massive beasts out over those hills and valleys and rocks and river-beds, seven hundred miles to their new home, requires the highest hunting and tracking skill, and courage, patience, endurance, sweat, muscle, initiative and dedication to the cause of wildlife conservation.

This book is not a documentary history of Rhodesia's Operation Rhino, it is the story of it. It is a true story, rendered more dramatic by a soothsayer's prediction that death and bloody injury would accompany the Operation, and I have tried to write it truly, as a story, as I witnessed it and as the rest was told to me.

John Gordon Davis
November 1970

Dramatis Personae

(or List of Characters)
in order of appearance

JOHN GORDON DAVIS European, early thirties, brown hair, narrator.

RONALD THOMPSON European, early thirties, blond hair, Warden, expert in Black Rhino, fiery; shares leadership for the Operation with Paul Coetsee.

NORMAN PAYN European, early fifties, black hair, veteran Ranger, expert detective, quiet.

BRIGHTSPARK TAFURANDIKA African, early sixties, short black curly hair, narrator's servant, very fond of alcoholic beverages, loquacious.

BEN African, early fifties, short black curly hair, Thompson's personal tracker and assistant.

GRAHAM HALL European, early thirties, brown hair, Ranger, quiet.

RICHARD PEEK European, early twenties, blond hair, Ranger, zestful.

NEVIN LEES-MAY European, early twenties, blond hair, Ranger, reserved.

PAUL COETSEE   European, early thirties, blond hair, Warden, renowned hunter, shares leadership of the Operation with Thompson, very self-controlled: the man who consulted the soothsayer.

KAPESA   African, early forties, short black curly hair, Coetsee's personal tracker and assistant.

JOHN OSBORNE   European, early thirties, dark hair, Ranger, very good-natured.

DAVID SCAMMEL   European, mid-twenties, brown hair, Ranger, zestful.

Others

INTRODUCTION

ALL the rivers were dry at this time of the year, except this one, and here where the wild animals came to drink it flowed very slowly, in small rocky sandy pools, and the rocks and the white river sand banks were hot. The game trail through the hot dry silent bush led to this place in the river.

Two of the line of snares which the African poacher set at this drinking place were concealed on the game trail. They all had the *mushonga*, the witch-doctor's blessing, to bring luck and to prevent any other poacher from stealing them. They were big nooses made of stout wire cable three-eighths of an inch thick. One snare was suspended, a neck noose, and below it was set the other, a foot noose. The end of the neck snare was lashed to a heavy log which the poacher had chopped down, and the foot snare was lashed to a mopani tree beside the trail.

That hot quiet African sundown the rhinoceros cow and her calf came to drink. The cow was five feet six inches tall at the shoulder and she weighed two thousand pounds, and the calf following her was three months old and thirty inches tall. She came down the trail, great agile armoured strength, cautious in front of her calf, but she did not see the snares. She lumbered her great hind-foot into the ground snare and her head went through the neck noose. As she felt the nooses drag on her she snorted and lunged to shake them off and the nooses dragged tight and bit into her neck and hind-foot, and she roared and plunged and went mad.

She lunged forward and the cables bit deep and the tree shook and her roar was half-strangled in her throat, the cables cut down through her thick hide and the blood came, they

15

crunched her great windpipe and cut down into the sinews of her hind-leg as she lunged. She went mad and bellowed, strangled, and flung her neck and great horned head and her eyes rolled red and terrified, and the cables cut deep. She reared up and shook her great terrified head and the heavy log the neck noose was lashed to jerked about, she roared and bellowed and bucked her great back and lunged and the cables bit deeper and she fell, tripped on her great bleeding hind-leg wrenched out bloody behind her. She crashed on to her huge chest and over on to her side, great feet thrashing and the dust flew and the earth shook. She scrambled up, she lunged to escape exactly as the poacher knew she would and the wires wrenched deeper; she crashed again and the earth shook, she wrenched her neck and leg against the wire, she reared up on her hind-legs and thrashed the air with her great hooves and threw her head, she tried to get her foot to the wire stretched from her neck to stamp it away but she could not reach it and she crashed again, she tried to hook the wire with her horn, and she could not, and she thrashed round and lunged her great horn at the wire holding her hind leg, and the neck noose jerked her head back, and she crashed again, rasping her bellow, and the nooses pulled tighter. And all the time the calf made small darts and dashes round her, small hooves scrambling and his ears cocked forward all the time, scrambling and darting and falling over his feet in his anxiety and fear, and all the time he made startled miaowing whimpering noises, terrified, around his great thrashing mother. All the animals coming down to the river to drink heard the great thrashing and the wrenching and the strangled snorting, they flicked their ears and sniffed the air for the danger, stamping their feet agitatedly and milling; they drank quickly and turned and made off back into the bush. For ten minutes the big cow thrashed and roared and crashed, red-eyed, and the dust flew and the tree shook and the big log jerked and the wires snared deep, and she was mad for breath. Ten minutes and the foot snare snapped off from the tree.

It snapped suddenly and she fell, she scrambled up wild-eyed and lunged down the game trail dragging the log by the tight noose in her neck. She blundered on gasping and wheezing and the calf galloped after her and the log bounced after her. She threw her great strangled head trying to shake off the snare tight in her neck. Crashing and thundering and blundering and from her hind-foot trailed the broken snare, embedded deep. She crashed through the bush away from the river, up the side of the hill and down the other side, and she plunged straight over into a gully crashing and falling and the rocks crashing with her, and the calf fell down after her, squealing, she scrambled to her feet and ran again, and the log bounced dragging behind her, jerking and catching on the rocks and the bushes, and each time the snare jerked tighter. For ten minutes she ran making a great noise trying to get away from the torment, and the calf galloped stumbling behind her, ears back, ten minutes she ran through the bush, going slower and slower, gasping and scrambling, then the log did what it was meant to do, it jammed between rocks and wrenched her by the neck, and she collapsed.

She tried to heave herself up, heaving gasping against the tight wire, trembling, trying to get up, and her wild red eyes bulging and her nostrils and mouth wide open, straining, gasping, and the blood running down her neck and welling up out of her leg; she tried and the wire round her neck jerked her back cutting deeper each time, and she could not, and then she just collapsed there flat out on her knees and her neck stretched tight against the wire snare. She lay there, black prehistoric beast, strangling, trembling, great ribbed flanks heaving for breath and her nostrils wide open and her mouth wide open making her strangled sucking noises and her wild exhausted eyes bulging red, and her noise was very loud in the silence of the sunset.

The small calf stood panting beside her in the darkness, bleeding where he had fallen galloping frantic after her. He milled, panting, his long ears twitching all the time for the danger. He puffed about his great fallen mother, and he made his miaowing noises of distress. He had not yet had his drink of water for the day. The small calf milled and miaowed and flicked his long ears back and forth listening for danger a long time, and then he settled down to this new situation, and he wanted to drink. He came nudging and miaowing up to her great belly, looking for her teats. The cow lay strangling, and the calf knelt down on his front knees with his ears flat back, and she was too low for him and so he got down on his stomach and nudged his head under her hind-legs and he managed to get hold of one teat, and he stared sucking.

The moon came up and she lay there, flanks heaving silver in the moonlight and the blood running black from her neck and hind-leg, rasping, gasping, and the calf making his sucking noises. The noose was cutting deep screwing up her windpipe, but after a while she got some breath back. The noose round her hind-foot was embedded down at the bone. The pain started now that she was collapsed, the great searing throbbing at the tight wire deep in her leg and her neck. It would take her a long time to die.

In the moonlight the hyenas came. Crouching in the moon-light through the bush, they shifted around, smelling the blood, knowing but not yet daring, particularly watching the calf. The calf heard them and he smelt them and he made his miaowing noises, his head was up all the time; he turned back and forth and round his dam looking and listening, his ears going all the time. He was very frightened, but if any creature came to touch his mother he would attack fiercely, charging with his very small horn which was only half an inch long now.

The big cow eventually heard the hyenas also through her strangling and the great pain, and she tried to scramble up to turn about to face them, and she released the tension on the wire and the log came loose from the rocks. She stumbled back over the rocks head down blindly, gasping and trying to roar at the hyenas and only making rasping noises because of the noose tight deep down in her neck. She fell down the dark rocks on her knees and she clambered up and stumbled on, the blood running from her neck and foot, and the calf followed her.

The big cow staggered, blindly, gasping through the moonlit bush, head down, and the big log followed behind her jerking and catching and dragging the wire tighter into her neck, as it was supposed to do, and the hyenas followed. She was dragging her hind-foot, it buckled with the wire tight around the bone because all the muscles were severed, she lurched and then dragged the foot forward again, then buckled again. The calf stumbled after her. She was going slowly now, slower and slower staggering and buckling and crashing and falling and all the time making her great strangled sucking noises. All through the long moonlit night the big cow staggered, dragging the log. She was very thirsty, big prehensile mouth open gasping, but she was only thinking of getting away from the strangling. The blood was a big black running sheen on her massive neck in the moonlight, and on her buckling hind-foot.

By the dawn the infection had set in, great swollen stabbing throbbing agony now. Her thirst was very bad. Sometimes she was unconscious when she fell down, then the gasping brought her round, and the stabbing throbbing, the massive black pounding inside her head, and the big pounding of her heart. But it would still take her a long time to die. Not today, in the heat, nor even tonight, maybe not even tomorrow nor tomorrow night. Not until the gangrene poisoned her whole massive body with its black-green pounding agony, unless she strangled herself. Unless the lions came. Or maybe unless the hyenas came. Or unless the poacher came, tracking her big marks where she dragged the log, and speared her. But the poacher was a long way away, at his beerdrink. It would take a long time for her to die.

By first light the big cow only knew that she had to have water, she was heading for the water, big black dying beast staggering and buckling on her hind-leg so her whole great black back jerked and the big deep red wound round her neck sprang open each time and her eyes bulging mad red. And the calf stumbled after her.

It was high noon when she got near the water. She could smell it, big nostrils wide open and great dry mouth stretched open, and the calf smelt it also. Down the long, hot, dry, yellow, grey, brown bush the big cow came, dragging and rasping and falling, with the great thirst and the agony. Seven hundred yards, and after a long time six hundred, and after longer five hundred, four hundred, and through her craze she could smell the water clearly now.

When she was two hundred yards from the water the log jammed again. It caught between two trees. The wire jerked, and she fell, and she kicked her great legs to get up and threw her maddened head, kicked and threw again and again beating the ground to get up and get down there to the water, but they were slow exhausted thumps and crashes now. Then she lay there stretched out flat on her side with the deep wire stretching tight from her neck and her great flanks heaving and her mouth and nostrils wide open; she could not get up. The infection was a big bleeding suppurating hump round her strangling neck now, and her hind-foot was gaping down to the bone.

All that long hot day the big rhinoceros cow lay there near the water. Sometimes she tried to get up. Sometimes she did make it up, and she tried to go forward on her three legs and the noose stopped her and cut deeper and she lurched hard against it, crazed, head down straining against the wire, rasping for air and the water, and then she crashed down again. Sometimes she was nearly unconscious. But she was rasping in just enough air, and the great pain brought her round, and then she tried to get up again, and crashed down again. The flies were thick on her eyes, and her mouth and her great swollen neck and foot wounds

20

now. Then the ants came, the big black Matabele ants, coming to the smell of blood. The calf stayed with her, making his miaowing noises. He was very frightened and very thirsty for water, but he dared not go to drink without the cow. Sometimes he lay down beside her, flat on his belly, and sucked. Sometimes he lay down beside her and even slept. But most of the time he shuffled about her, head up and looking and his ears going all the time, and miaowing, and he was very thirsty. In the late afternoon the gangrene set in in the big cow's neck and hind-foot and the greatest agony started. But the big cow would still take a long time to die.

That night the calf went down to the water to drink. He had not had water for forty-eight hours. He waited a long time wanting the water very badly and smelling it, and his ears going all the time. He made many false starts. He started, head up and ears going, listening and smelling the water. He trod care-fully through the bush, stopping the starting and making his hesitant anxious miaowing noises, and looking back at his great mother, then putting his ears back when she did not get up and then straight away twitching in all directions again, looking round. Many times he got a little way like this and then he suddenly turned and ran back to his dam, and then stood dry panting beside her great body, looking and listening. The moon came up.

After many such false starts he got a long way from his mother, looking everywhere in the moonlight, and smelling the water and smelling the night and stopping and starting, down through the silver-gold-black bush towards the water, he could only hear his mother's groaning a long way back, his heart was pounding but the dry thirst was worse than the fear, he got to where he could even glimpse the water shining in the moon-light, and the hyenas got him.

The hyenas had been watching for a long time, they had kept downwind of him, and when he was nearly at the water they came at him. Came crouching running out of the bush, racing each other to the kill, he heard them and spun around and started to run squealing back to his mother two hundred yards away and the hyenas raced low at him in the moonlight, he ran squealing scrambling as fast as his legs would carry him and one hyena leapt, tore at his haunches and got his small curled tail and tore it clean off but he was running so desperately terrified hard he only felt the squealing scrambling frantic terror, the yellow teeth ripped at his squealing heels, fleeting scrambling flat out through the moonlight screaming for his mother, the snarling murderous hyenas raced snapping after him, he got half-way back to his mother, and they got him. One leapt on his neck and the other got his hind-leg and the third got his foreleg, he bucked and twisted and screamed and thrashed and they hung on deep-fanged and pulled him down, hung on, he tried to scramble up and run run run, but they were all over him, biting and tearing and snarling, and they got at his screaming throat, and hung on and shook and tore and wrenched all over him in the moonlight, they got down to his windpipe and they tore his windpipe open and out and they killed him. And there and then they tore him up and ate him. The big cow heard it all, she knew what was happening and she tried to get up and charge, she scrambled her big legs and threw her great head beating the earth, she got half-way up and crashed down making wild rasping noises, she tried again and again wild-eyed and trying to bellow to her calf and charge at the hyenas, she kept trying all the time they were killing him, and while they were tearing him apart, and while they were cracking his bones in their jaws and eating him, and she kept trying long after they had left his bloody skeleton and loped off back into the night; she tried all that night scrambling her great legs and pounding her great head and trying to bellow, but she could not get up. After a long time she just lay there dying, making her great rasping noises, and her heart was breaking.

But she did not die that night. Nor the next morning, nor the next long dry thirst-crazed afternoon, with the ants and the flies. That afternoon the oxpecker birds came and pecked into her neck and her leg, eating her. That afternoon the vultures came, circling down, and they flapped into the trees and flapped on the ground waiting for her to die. Late that night she died in the moonlight, from the strangulation and the thirst and the agony and the poison and the exhaustion. No creature came to help her die, no poacher, no god. The poacher was still at his beerdrink and God was elsewhere.

Part One

CHAPTER ONE

FOR the first two months of Operation Rhino they were working from a base camp at Mususumoya, in the Umfurudzi. The first month Thompson and Coetsee led the operation jointly. The second month Thompson returned to his post in the Gona-re-Zhou and Coetsee led the operation alone. Altogether they captured seventeen rhino and translocated them six hundred miles; there were still a few left, but they had become very wild, so at the end of that second month the base camp was moved and Coetsee went back to his post in the Zambesi Valley, while Thompson prepared to come back and take over. The two men were sharing the leadership in this way in order to pool their knowledge and simultaneously to acquire experience concurrently in this unusual and dangerous exercise.

Thompson was an excellent hunter and an academic expert on rhinos, as far as anybody can be an expert on such a rare and dangerous beast, about which very little has been written; he was preparing a thesis on them. Coetsee had been a professional hunter a great deal of his life; he was one of the best hunters in Africa: he and Thompson benefited a lot from each other sharing the leadership. And in the event of one of them getting a rhino horn through his gut, the other could carry on.

So at the end of that second month, Richard Peek and Graham Hall moved the base camp three hundred miles to Nyamasota, in the Ruya, where they built a new rhino stockade.

Old Norman Payn preceded them and set up his new reconnaissance camp twenty miles away and sent out his game scouts to assess the area. Everything was ready when Thompson arrived at the beginning of the third month to take over again, and I met him for the first time.

Coetsee I had known quite well before, from the Zambesi Valley days and I had heard all about Thompson, who was the Department of Wildlife's blue-eyed boy. Indeed, his eyes were very blue, his hair was blond and he was good-looking in a youthful way, and he spoke with a soft English accent. He wasn't speaking softly on his arrival, however, because he was a day late, because the game scout who was supposed to guide him through the bush to the new camp had lost his way eight times. In addition the same scout had dropped Thompson's camera and then sat heavily on his carton of eggs. Thompson did not like scrambled eggs very much and he *did* like his camera very much, he did not like wasting a whole day of the taxpayers' money; and finally, the eighth time, he had unloaded the game scout from the Landrover with instructions to improve his tracking by diligent practice, starting from now, like finding the camp on foot, and Thompson had found his own way into the Ruya. Thompson was not speaking softly at all on arrival but he inspected the good camp and stockade that young Richard and Graham Hall had made; and we told him about all the rhino spoor Old Norman had found and other news that men with rhinos in their hearts like to hear, and he read the reports that Coetsee had written on Mususumoya; somebody gave him a beer and he settled down in front of his tent, and started loading darts with the M99 drug for tomorrow, and he cheered up.

In the late winter, way up there in the Ruya, on the Rhodesian border with Mozambique, in Chief Masoso's country, the great bush is dry and the earth is hard dry and the cattle are thin. In the night it is cold and in the day the sun shines hot out

26

of a mercilessly blue sky. All the river-beds are dry, the Mudzi and the Bungwe and the Shamba; all dry except the Ruya winding through the hot, grey rocks, through the hot bush; and along the hot sand and rock banks the tall reeds were green.

All the animals that were left came down to the Ruya to drink; the rhino and the wart-hog and the lion and all the buck and the cattle. Most of the animals were gone, snared by the poachers, both Chief Masoso's people and the itinerant poachers, the men who came for a while from far away with their snares and their old muzzle-loaders. The elephant had all left, because of the poachers, and most of the buck were already snared, and because of that most of the lion had gone, although we knew there were still four lion, one very large and two rather young, because we had seen their spoor. And most of the rhino had been snared. But there were still twelve left around the Ruya, possibly sixteen, according to the spoor. The natives said that right on the border, where the Ruya was called the Luia, there was a very big, bad-tempered bull who lived by himself, very dangerous; and they swore that he was white in colour. They even said his eyes were pink.

We were very interested to think that we might have an albino rhinoceros – the first albino rhino in the world – but we did not believe he was really white. It was probably the colour of the mud in the mud-bath which only he used, and his pink eyes were probably bloodshot from anger, for nothing makes a rhino madder than being got close enough to to have the colour of his eyes seen. There were a number of other big bad bulls which had treed our scouts, and a number of cows with calves, and two of the calves were very small, maybe not more than one month old, according to their spoor. The poachers would get them. In two years there would be none left. The poachers would put them to the long, bad death of the snare, and dry the meat and hides and sell them, and sell the rhino horn for a few pounds to the traders, who would sell it to the middlemen down the coast, who would ship it all over the world to be sold at very high prices indeed as an aphrodisiac. Soon there would be no more rhino in the Ruya.

Our base camp was on a long, low hill. There were five encampments, spaced well apart in the tall yellow grass and the mopani trees. In the middle in a clearing, was the office, which was a tarpaulin suspended taut between two trees, with a long trestle table and maps, documents and stores. Parked behind it was the Land-Rover with the two-way radio that could reach all over Rhodesia. In this clearing was the main camp-fire, big logs that smouldered all day and night, and near the fire, under a tree, was the kitchen table made of branches wired together, and all the pots and pans and even a big, old, black, iron wood stove. Each of us had our own cookboy and our own fire at our own tent, but frequently we ate together round the big fire, in which case everyone brought his own food and his own cookboy with him.

The sleeping-tents were pitched on both sides of the clearing, at different distances off into the grass and trees; and something of the character of each man was discernible in each chosen location. Closest to the clearing was Thompson's tent, which also held all the drugs and darts, guns and medicines, as well as his research papers. Richard had pitched his tent closest to Thompson and to the clearing. Richard was a tall, lean, keen and zestful young ranger, with a shock of brown hair and eager eyes, who was Thompson's protégé and he just loved this life in general and catching rhinos in particular. If you had asked what he wanted for his birthday, young Richard would have answered, 'To catch a rhino by myself.' Neither Thompson nor Coetsee had yet allowed him to go in alone and dart a rhino, but Thompson had promised him that this month he might, depending on the progress and the situation of the beast at the time. It takes a lot of time and manpower and money to make contact with one rhino. It is also very dangerous and you cannot afford mistakes. Richard was devouring all he could learn from

28

everybody, and he pitched his tent as close as he did in case he missed anything.

Considerably further away from the clearing, into the tall grass, was young Nevin's tent. He was tall and blond and shy. He was the most junior ranger on the operation; he seldom spoke, even round the camp-fire. He just listened. It was doubtful whether he would be given the chance this year of going in alone to dart a rhino, which disappointed him, but he did not show it.

On the opposite side of the clearing, well into the grass, were Graham Hall's tents, more elaborate than anybody's. He had two tents and a plaited grass fence for additional privacy. He had been a professional hunter, he said that only a fool was uncomfortable in the bush. He was Thompson's and my age, but still a ranger, having only recently joined the Department. He knew what he was doing in the bush, what he said and did was always good sense, and Thompson and Coetsee relied on him.

And considerably beyond Hall's tents, farthest of all from the clearing, was my encampment. I was the observer, the chronicler, and the idea was that I should not be disturbed, nor my typewriter disturb them, if I had the strength at the end of a day to use it.

Beyond our hill the mopani trees stretched out in all directions, with many hills, on and on for ever, all the way to the horizon; and the yellow grass and the grey trees turned mauve out there. Two miles away was Mozambique, where the river Ruya became the Luia and there was a hill with a beacon on it, marking the border. Behind the base camp to the south was our stockade for holding the rhino pending their translocation to the Gona-re-Zhou game reserve, seven hundred miles away to the south, where they would be safe from poachers. It was a stout, square stockade, twelve feet tall, made out of mopani logs lashed together vertically with wire on to a cross-membered framework of logs, and it was quartered into four pens. The stockade could be opened by pulling out certain logs, and similarly each pen could be opened into the next, to get a rhino from one to another. It was a very good stockade. Behind it were the big Mercedes recovery vehicle and other lorries and many forty-four gallon drums of the fuel that Great Britain was supposed to be blockading; there was the water bowzer for us and the rhinos and, under tarpaulins, scores of sacks of mealie meal and groundnuts for the African staff. Beyond these things were the camps of the game scouts, very neat with their Departmental issue; and beyond them again were the fireplaces of the locally-hired labourers, Chief Masoso's people, who slept anyhow they liked. Maybe forty miles beyond, to the south-east as the crow flies, was a mission station, but apart from the missionaries there were supposed to be no other Europeans in the area.

But now, at the end of the first day of Thompson's late arrival, after he had begun to get over the game scout and the camera and the sat-on-eggs, we heard the big Government bulldozer working somewhere far away over the Ruya hills, where we were going to be stalking rhino, and that set him off again. It set everybody off. That sunset old Norman Payn drove the twenty miles from his camp on the river Ruya to ours to complain bitterly to Thompson about it. Old Norman was bespectacled and short and dark and very suntanned, a veteran ranger who had always steadfastly resisted promotion lest he had to leave the bush for a desk, and he was an expert and dedicated detective of poachers. Once upon a time, long ago, he had also been a professional hunter. He was a very tough and gentle elderly man who very seldom swore, but he was swearing ungently about the bulldozer. Shortly afterwards the European in charge of the bulldozer drove the fifteen miles from his camp to visit us; he was very pleased to have heard of other white men in the area. We gave him a beer, very Britishly, and we settled down round the fire to cook our fresh steaks in our shovels;

Thompson had brought the steaks from Mount Darwin because, in order to set a good example to Chief Masoso's people we were not shooting for the pot; we cooked the steaks in our shovels because naturally every man in the bush has a shovel and they are more convenient to use round a camp-fire than a frying-pan; as soon as we had got down to this, we started to pick on the bulldozer man. Thompson cleared his throat and said:

'Why must you work your bloody bulldozer round here, just when we're trying to capture rhino, old chap?'

'I've got my orders,' the bulldozer man said, surprised and defensive.

'And I've got *my* orders,' Thompson said. 'To capture rhino.'

'You can still catch your rhino,' the bulldozer man said, mystified; 'these hills are big enough for both of us.'

'These hills are *not* big enough,' Thompson said, trying to be polite. 'How can I capture rhino with your bloody great bulldozer chomping round making all that offensive noise?'

'But my bulldozer's working fifteen–twenty miles away!' the bulldozer man pointed injuredly out beyond the firelight.

'That's about twenty miles too close,' Thompson said. 'The sound carries. It frightens the rhinos away and we've got to find them.'

'Well,' said the man, trying to look on the bright side and maybe, but not probably, trying to make a joke, 'the noise of my bulldozer will stifle the sound of your footsteps.'

Thompson stared at him. We all stared at him.

'I don't think you understand, old chap,' Thompson said, trying to be polite.

'I've got my orders.' The bulldozer man blinked. 'These roads must be made so that the natives can develop their lands. It's a matter of National Importance,' he said, pronouncing the capitals.

'And saving the rhino from extermination is a matter of

International Importance,' said Thompson, also with capitals. 'Do you know what man is doing? Do you know what the likes of you and your bloody bulldozers are doing to nature and wildlife all over the world?'

'It's not *my* bulldozer,' the man said, trying to be reasonable. 'There must be Progress.' With a capital.

'Just let me get my rhino safely out of here first,' Thompson said; 'And you can bulldoze your Progress to Timbuktu. To kingdom come if you like.'

'And when you get to the sea,' Old Norman said, 'please don't stop.'

'Progress?' Graham Hall said. 'Pollution!'

Thompson pointed out into the vast bush blackness beyond the firelight.

'Two miles over there is Portuguese Mozambique. By International Law we can't follow them if they cross the border. Right?' He appealed to me.

'Right,' I said, loyally, although I seemed to remember some case somewhere about the right of whalermen to pursue a whale from international waters into another country's territorial waters, 'and I used to be a lawyer.'

'High-class Department, this,' Graham Hall said – 'take our own lawyers along. He's also a writer,' Graham Hall went on. 'He'll write horrid things about you and the whole world will hate you.'

'Can one Government Department sue another Government Department?' old Norman asked menacingly.

'Yes,' I said.

'That's it, then,' Graham Hall said. 'Take out a summons then write about it in the *News of the World*.'

'So?' the bulldozer man said, unamused, and appealing to us all to be reasonable. 'Let the Portuguese have them. Rhinos belong to everybody.'

We were all shocked.

Thompson tried to stay polite.

'Old man, once they go into Mozambique those rhinos are dead. The Portuguese have less control over poachers than we have.'

'But maybe they won't run towards Mozambique.' The bulldozer man pointed out the bright side. He had been very pleased to hear we were in the area, he had come a long way to be sociable, but as soon as he found us, what happened? 'Maybe they'll run that way.' He pointed south, optimistically. We were all shaking our heads, but we left it to Thompson.

'Please.' Thompson leant back in his camp chair, exasperated but trying not to glare at the bulldozer man, who was his guest and who, after all, was just a civil servant like himself. 'Do you know what money it costs to catch one rhino? Do you know what it costs the Rhodesia Government and the generous public to move me and my men and our equipment way up here so that we can translocate a dozen rhino for mankind, so they won't be tortured to death, so that the world will have rhino? Do you know? Well,' Thompson nodded, trying not to look angry with his guest. 'It costs three hundred pounds per rhino.'

The bulldozer man was on his mettle.

'And have *you* any idea what it costs the Rhodesia Government to send me and a bulldozer and all my equipment and a road gang out here to make roads so the natives and the National Economy can develop?' he said injuredly with appropriate capitals.

'Please,' Thompson said again. 'Just let me get my rhino out.'

'And what am I supposed to do with my bulldozer and road gang while you're catching rhinos?' the bulldozer man said.

'I know what you can do with your bulldozer,' Graham Hall said.

I felt a little sorry for the bulldozer man. He was just another nice enough chap stuck out in the bush. It wasn't his fault his vocation lay with bulldozers.

33

'I have my orders,' the bulldozer man said again.

'And I have mine.' Thompson tried to smile.

We all sat there, embarrassed.

'What we'll do,' Thompson said, 'is I'll get on to the radio to my Ministry and you get on to your radio to your Ministry and let them fight it out.'

'In their underpants,' I said, trying to make a joke for the sake of the bulldozer man.

CHAPTER TWO

WHEN the sun comes up flaming red over the hard bush hills, the tall dry grass is at first a fleeting golden-mauve and then it is soft yellow and the world is very still and beautiful; in the long, cold, gold-mauve, inching early-morning shadows it is the best time. My tents were a hundred yards away from Thompson's camp and I could not see it because of the tall yellow grass, but I could just hear him talking on the radio to old Norman about spoor. I called to Brightspark Tafurandika to make coffee and I got no answer. I left my sleeping-tent and went round the back to the dining-tent. He was asleep at the fire, wrapped in his groundsheet. He had not lain on the bed of grass he had cut.

'Tafurandika!'

He sat up. He was an old man with his two front teeth missing and his eyes were blodshot; he looked terrible.

'Where did you go last night?'

Brightspark Tafurandika put a hand on his head and waved his other hand at the horizon.

'Already you have found where the beer is!' The nearest huts must have been several miles away, but Tafurandika homed in on such huts like a camel on an oasis. He even looked like a camel. 'Are you a scamenga? Ah! too much! Are you a tsotsi? Ah! you are many tsotsis! What are you?' I was speaking Chilapalapa.

'I am an old man.' Brightspark Tafurandika held his head. 'A frail old man.'

'When I hired you you said you were as strong as a buffalo with the heart of a lion and the eyes of an eagle. But all you have is the thirst of a fish!'

'I don't drink myself,' Brightspark Tafurandika said.

'Make me coffee, Fish-That-Does-Not-Drink.'

I went back to my sleeping-tent. When the Employment Officer down at the Labour Exchange in Salisbury had paraded on Brightspark Tafurandika I had said in English: 'Haven't you got anybody less discouraging?' 'Nkosi,' Tafurandika had said in Chilapalapa, 'I am a great cook and a fearless hunter.' 'We will be catching rhinos,' I said. 'Alive. There will be no fresh meat.' 'You'll be catching *what*?' Tafurandika said, 'Chipimbiri,' I said. 'My children are still at school,' Brightspark Tafurandika said, 'I have responsibilities.'

When I was drinking the coffee, and the sun was just half-way over the horizon and the sky was riotously beautiful, red and orange flaming out into the still, clear, clean night grey and there were still some stars in the dark blue of the west, and the tops of the grey mopani trees to the west were just lighting up into early gold and when my mopani trees to the east were just starting to flame skeletal black against the sunrise, on fire on their edges, and the first gold was beginning to glow in the mauve-yellow tops of the elephant grass, now, at this best time of the early morning, with my first mug of coffee and cigarette, there came this shout from Thompson down at his tents:

Chipimbiiiiri!

And I stood up and shouted for Brightspark Tafurandika to bring me oranges; I stuffed a handful of glucose sweets in my pocket and gulped down the rest of my coffee as fast as I could;

35

then I started through the tall yellow grass towards the stock-ade and the vehicles. The sun was not yet clear of the trees. I could hear Thompson shouting at the natives we had hired locally. When I got there the natives were climbing up on to the big high back of the Mercedes five-tonner and Thompson was glaring at them, very angry.

'Would you believe it?' Thompson snapped at me. 'They were all out on a beerdrink all night; not one of them has slept.'

The natives were grinning and you could smell the Kaffir beer and old sweat.

Thompson shouted in Chilapalapa: *'Hurry up! Today you will suffer out there in the sun, my fine men! Today you will curse the beer! And remember when your heads suffer greatly that it is your faults and not mine!'*

Thompson was disgusted. First the game scout, then the bulldozer, now the bloody beerdrink. Ben was taking his time climbing up on to the truck. Ben was the most important one, the best tracker – Thompson's personal tracker; his big, floppy hat over his eyes, he was puffing his pipe, surly. Ben always looked surly. He very seldom said anything. He just tracked. Thompson glared but didn't shout at Ben. Ben sat down on the lorry with his back to everybody, then stared over Thompson's head, puffing his pipe. He knew he was the most important one, hang-over or no hang-over. Thompson shouted:

'And if any man fails to do his work today, if any man fails to keep up because of his babelaazi and that man shall walk back to camp tonight, truly, and may the lions devour him!'

Most of them were up on the truck now, clambering around to sit down, looking hung-over, some looking bad, some grin-ning, some sheepish, some happy drunk.

'Do you know what we are here for?' Thompson shouted. *'Do you know why we employ you? Are you men? No, you are women! Are you responsible people? No you are many chil-dren, truly! Ah!'*

He gave them a final glare and turned and strode round to the cab and climbed in and slammed the door. I put my foot up to the big back wheel and heaved myself up on to the back of the big truck with the natives and Graham Hall and Richard and Nevin, and the big engine started. Now the boss was gone all the natives were jabbering happily. The smell of Kaffir beer and sweat was very strong, and it was cold.

The sun was just clear of the trees, golden with long, mauve, early-morning shadows and it was cold on the back of the big lorry churning down the bush road. The cold cut through my sweaters, the natives' black skin goosefleshed; I could no longer smell them. The big lorry threw up much dust, mauve and golden, billowing up behind us and hanging still in the cold sunrise. The natives were still full of beer, noisy. The road wound up and down over the long bush hills. Sometimes we passed kraals near the road, three, four pole and dagga-thatched huts round a dust-trampled clearing with a pen for the *mombes*, the cattle, made of branches and sticks, and a mud and thatch grain bin, and some Kaffir chickens scratching and some-times some pigs and always some very skinny Kaffir dogs, and the cooking fires were smouldering, and some women and chil-dren who looked up, stared and usually waved to us in the African way, shy and surprised to see us and our big lorry, and we waved and the natives on the lorry shouted, *We are going to catch chipimbiri*, and laughing, they felt very superior riding on the back of the big dusting lorry and most of them were still happy from the all-night beerdrink. But the kraals were few and far between and mostly it was just the vast, thick, grey-brown bush, Africa, the dirt road, the bush and the sky and the early sun and the dust behind us. Down in the shadows of the valleys it was very cold, you could see the shadowed cold coming ahead down there and then the cold valley hit you and you hoped that Mkondo, the driver, would find the road so bad at the bottom that he would have to slow right down to change

gears, right down so the grey shadow wind would stop just a
moment, and, when he did stop suddenly you felt very warm by
contrast and it was suddenly bliss, then immediately it got less
blissful again as he churned up the other side of the gulley; then
he got up the gulley into the sun and the early golden sun
suddenly on your body counteracted the gathering momentum
and you loved the sun; then Mokondo gathered speed and the
sun was no longer any good against the wind. We went up a
long hill and the native next to me who was called Gasoline
pointed his black gooseflesh arm suddenly and I saw two kuda
standing, an adult and a half-grown calf. 'Nyama!' Gasoline
shouted happy drunk.

The kudu looked at us, then bounded away into the bush and
they were gone.

'Are they good to eat?' I asked Gasoline above the wind.

'Ah! very good!' Gasoline beamed at me happily in the wind.
'Nyama!'

'Do you often eat them in this country?' I shouted.

'Ah! very often!' Gasoline boasted.

'Are they easy to catch?' I shouted.

'Ah! very easy when you know!' Gasoline boasted, delighted
with himself.

'How do you catch them?'

'I catch them with—' Gasoline stopped and looked at me.

'With snares? Or with guns?'

'No,' Gasoline said, 'I just find them dead.'

'Hey-hey,' I said, 'I caught you. I shall have to tell Nkosi
Thompson about you.'

'I only find them dead,' Gasoline said sheepishly. 'Truly.'

'Hey-hey,' I said, 'truly? Ah!'

The Mercedes turned off the track between two fields, the
fields hard and dry waiting for the rains, and went down the hill,
bouncing, on this even rougher track The sun was well up now
but it was still very cold. There were many branches hanging
over the road, branches that would knock your head open and

throw you off the truck and we had to duck as we bounded underneath them. There were more kraals now and more natives looking up, staring, surprised, and children came running to see us, grinning and waving. *'We are going to catch chipimbiri alive!'* our natives shouted happily and they laughed as the people stared. It was a kind of joke, to make the people stare uncomprehendingly; if they heard, they did not believe that we were going to catch chipimbiri alive, nobody can catch chipimbiri alive, not even the white men. The truck went down a long rough hill and thick bush, and came to a dry river-bed and Mkondo put the big Mercedes into four-wheel drive and he revved and rushed the thick, dry, white sand and the dry dust rose and we bounced and churned across the steep, dry bank where we could see the tracks of Old Norman's Land-Rover, and churned, roaring, bouncing, dusting, crashing, up the other side, racing the engine to keep up the momentum, swinging hard round the trees, ducking for the overhead branches. The sun was well up now but it was still cold on the back of the bouncing lorry; and when we came down a long, naked, charred hill where the natives had burned the scrub for their ploughing, and there was the river Ruya down the low valley, wide, flat rocks and rivers and green reeds, and there was Old Norman's camp on the banks. The Mercedes bounced into the camp, and Old Norman came walking up through the golden grass to greet us, very brown and khaki and gentle and moustached and quietly-spoken. 'Good morning, good morning,' he said.

The natives clambered off the truck, still hung-over and a little drunk and went to squat under a big Msasa tree round the servants' fire. We went to Old Norman's fire on the river-bank and stood in the wispy smoky warmth of it in the sunshine and his cookboy brought us mugs of tea, and Old Norman told Thompson about the spoor he and his trackers had found out there. Old Norman had rhinos in his heart. Spoor all over the place, he said. There was also last night's spoor and yesterday morning's spoor all over the place, but, man, there was hang of a beautiful just this morning's spoor. Not three miles away. At least two calves. One calf very small, maybe only one month old. One very big bull. The radio in Old Norman's Land-Rover was calling back and forth, Wankie National Park reporting to Salisbury Head office about poachers. 'The bastards,' Thompson said.

'I'm on to some big poaching here too,' Old Norman confided.

'Yes?' I said.

'Just give me time. Let them think I'm stupid.'

'Guns or snares?' I said.

'Everything. In two years there won't be a single animal left in the Ruya,' Old Norman said.

'Catch the bastards,' Thompson said. 'Just catch them.' Our tea was finished.

'Right,' Thompson said.

We strode through the dry, golden, broken country in ragged single file, the game scout leading the way to the place where he had found the best spoor, then Thompson, then Richard, then Graham, then Nevin, then I, then the gun-bearers and the natives carrying the radio and the ropes and the water-bags and the axes. It was rough, broken country. After one hour the game scout stopped and pointed; we gathered round him, careful where we put our feet. There on the ground was the spoor. 'This is the first one,' the game scout said.

We crouched down and examined it. It was getting hot now and we were all sweating. There was a soft patch of dust and there was a faint depression which was the mark of one of the rhino's toes, and immediately next to it the tiny wrinkles of his pad.

'Leftmost toe.' Thompson picked up a twig and traced an outline round the spoor, clover-shaped, and the print of the whole foot came to life around the wrinkles.

40

'Kunene?' Thompson looked at Ben: 'This morning's?'

Ben nodded once, standing there, relaxed, indifferent, skinny, almost old, possibly hung-over but you couldn't tell, puffing his pipe.

'Where is the other spoor you found?'

'Over the hill,' the game scout pointed. 'Maybe two miles.'

'All right. We will follow this one.' It was eight o'clock.

CHAPTER THREE

HOT, the noon sky bright cloudless blue-white, and very little shade in the bare-tree bush. The hard, stony, rocky earth was hot under the rubber soles of our hockey boots, the hot, dry, still air was burning, hot, grey, brown bush and tall, dry, yellow grass, kopjies, big, grey rocky ridges and outcrops going on for ever, mauve, all the way to the blue-white skyline. This place was bad tracking country. The trackers were spread out, each going his own way, looking. We had lost the spoor again. A big troop of baboons had crossed the rhino's tracks and obliterated them. We had come a long way, over many hills and ravines round and about. We had recrossed our own tracks. The rhino had wandered a lot. You had to look for every sign in the book, just a flick of earth, a displaced pebble, a crushed dry leaf, a snapped twig maybe five feet off the ground where he had taken a passing mouthful.

No talking above a whisper was allowed. Everybody was spread out, hundreds of yards apart. Half of us were out of sight of each other. You lose sight of a man in any coloured clothing very quickly, a man in khaki more so. The native porters were sitting way back under a tree, waiting for us to find something. I was following Ben. Old head bent a little under his flopping Departmental felt hat, eyes bloodshot, pipe puffing, face impassive. His tin water-bottle suspended from his belt over his buttocks. Skinny black legs. Departmental boots, khaki leggings. I was following Ben because he was the best tracker and I was trying to learn something, improve my tracking. I would have given up way, way back, To recognize spoor is one thing, to interpret it is quite another. I could not tell age, unless it was obvious. I saw a sign, a dislodged stone, and I slapped my hip quietly to draw his attention and pointed. Ben's blodshot eyes flicked at it once.

'Zoro,' he said: Yesterday's.

Well, it looked all right to me. The underside of the stone looked pretty fresh to me. In this sun it could be today's. 'Why?' I whispered.

'Zoro,' said Ben.

I walked ten yards to his side and slightly behind him, so as not to tread on any sign before he had a chance to see it first. I saw another sign, a flattened leaf and you could see the edge of a toe on the ground beside it. I slapped my hip. Ben came over. He took one look at it and turned away ignoring it.

'Zoro?' I crouched down and examined it. How can you tell whether a dead dry leaf was crushed this morning or yesterday? In this sun. The small toe mark beside it was blurred certainly, but the ground was hard and dry. Very well. I heard the guinea-fowl whistle, *pherw-pherw*, the sound a man makes whistling against his finger and I looked up and I thought, thank God for that. It was coming from the north, downhill into the valley. We started towards it.

I saw Thompson and a tracker called Nyambi emerge out of bush a hundred yards to the south, heading towards the whistle. I hoped it wasn't Kalashaka who was calling us. Kalashaka, who carried the notebooks, fancied himself as a tracker but he wasn't a hell of a lot better than me. We converged through the tall hot grass on the whistle. It was Kalashaka, looking optimistic. Richard and Nevin were already there, examining the sign.

'Zoro,' Thompson said, disgusted Kalashaka looked crest-fallen. Ben came up leant his hand on his skinny knee and glanced at the sign. It was a small scrape on the hard earth.

'Kunene,' Ben said: This morning's.

Thompson looked at him, 'Zoro.': Yesterday's.

Ben shook his head imperceptibly.

'I am sure it's yesterday, truly,' Thompson said.

Ben was already gone, back turned, looking for the continuation of the sign. Kalashaka was beaming at himself. Thompson still crouched, examining the sign.

'Are you sure, Ben?'

Ben grunted without turning, eight paces off, looking.

'I think it's yesterday's,' Graham said.

Nevin didn't say anything. I didn't offer an opinion. I just hoped Ben was right. Thompson stood up.

'I guess he's right. He's always right.'

Already Ben and Nyambi and Kalashaka were spread out, twenty paces ahead under the hot dry sun, looking. Even the back of Kalashaka's head was beaming. We spread out and followed.

Down into the valley, over a deep gulley, up the other side, down to the river, along the bank, up into the hills, across a dry river-bed, back up into the hills: all the way it was hot and dry and hard. There was other spoor, but it was all *zoro*'s, yesterday's. We saw spoor of lion and kudu and impala, and those were today's, but all the rhino spoor was yesterday's, except the beast's we were following. We did not see any fresh dung. We lost it many times. We found where he had lain up in the midday heat, a dust-bowl next to an ant-heap under a thorn tree, the wrinkles of his hide imprinted in the dust. He had lain up there yesterday as well. We followed the spoor from this place up over the hill and down over a bad gulley and then

43

down again and across another dry river-bed. This animal was certainly moving around. We had walked twenty miles round and about. Thompson blamed it on the bulldozer working fifteen miles away. The sound carried. A lone bull should not range this far and wide. A cow with a calf will do it, to protect the calf, but a lone rhino should not. Thompson was pretty disgusted with life: with the hung-over natives, the bulldozer, the terrain, the spoor. 'Come on, *find* it!' From the second dry river-bed the spoor went up some very bad rocky country up into steep kopjies. The sign was very difficult to find, and it was looking old now. Maybe we had lost it and were now following yesterday's spoor. Then there was much old sign, yesterday's all over the place. And it was bad tracking country anyway. And baboon spoor. Baboons had jumped up and down all over it again.

'Yesterday's, today's and tomorrow's spoor,' Thompson said.

He worked up towards the top of the rise. Then he came striding down.

'That bloody bulldozer turned him. You can hear it from the top of the rise. He would have turned back when he heard it.'

We turned back through the baboon and the yesterday, today and tomorrow spoor. He would have headed in the opposite direction from the bulldozer, back down towards the dry river-bed. We spread wide out, heading back towards the river, looking for signs. We looked all along the long rugged dry bushy river-bank. Down into the river-bed. There was no spoor.

Thompson stopped in the river-bed under some shade. He gave the guinea-fowl whistle and we all came, plodding. Ben stood high up on the bank looking down at us, bloodshot eyes.

'It is because of your babbelaazi that we've lost it,' Thompson said. We were all sweating.

Ben just looked. Thompson glared at him. He was very fed up.

44

'It is very fortunate for you that you are not Nkosi Norman's person. Nkosi Norman would give you a good headache. I am too soft-hearted.'

Ben just looked.

'Are you suffering?'

Ben's shoulder just shrugged slightly once. He stood at the top of the bank.

'Do you know how much money we have wasted today? How much of the poor Government's money?'

Ben just looked. Ben didn't care a lump of baboon's dung about the poor Government's money.

'How much money of the poor tax-payer like me?' Thompson said.

Ben didn't care a lump of baboon's dung about the tax-payer either. He just stood there.

'It is three o'clock,' Thompson accused Ben. 'We have walked twenty miles. We have only two more hours of daylight. We do not even have spoor.'

Ben said, from the top of the bank, 'I will find it,' indifferently.

'Go,' Thompson glared at him. 'Go and find it. Go back to the yesterday, today and tomorrow place where we lost it. And don't come back until you have found it. And may your bab-belaazi pain you.'

Ben turned to go, indifferent. Nyambi turned to follow him.

'Ben,' Thompson called.

Ben stopped and looked back.

'Do you want a rest?'

Ben shook his head slightly once. He turned again, set off up the hill into the bush, a small, black, skinny, hard man in khaki, floppy hat, indifferent. Puffing his pipe.

We all sat down on the sand. The porters flopped down on the sand, stretched out, hung-over. You could smell the Kaffir beer sweat now. They were suffering.

45

'Roger-Roger,' Thompson said: wireless. The wireless porter opened his eyes and heaved himself up. The field radio was strapped to his back in a khaki canvas case. He plodded across the shade to Thompson, turned his back on him and sat down gratefully, presenting the radio on his back for Thompson's use.

'Aerial,' Thompson said.

The aerial porter was already there, hang-over and all. Thompson screwed it into the radio on Roger-Roger's back. He wiped his sweating face with his cap, switched on the machine, picked up the mouthpiece. 'Pooh,' he said to Roger-Roger sitting in front of him, 'you smell, truly.'

Roger-Roger grinned sheepishly at us, glistening with sweat, his back to Thompson.

'What did they put in that Kaffir beer?' Thompson said.

Roger-Roger grinned apologetically.

Thompson flicked on the transmission switch, resigned to the smell, and said sing-song:

'Four-one, four-one, four-one, four-one, four-one, mobile, over.' He flicked the switch on to receiving and we all listened.

There was some whining then a click and Old Norman's voice came over far way over the hills.

'Four-one, reading you strength three, over.'

'Roger, Norman,' Thompson took a tired breath: 'We're in a river-bed to hell and gone to—' he looked at the sun '—the south-west of your camp. Maybe fifteen miles. Do you read? Over.'

'Roger, you're in a river-bed about fifteen miles south-west of me, over.' The African porters were staring fascinated. They did not understand the English but they were listening, staring, sweating.

'I don't know what's happened to all those rhino you had tied up to a tree by their tails, but they have scattered to the four winds. I think the bulldozer alarmed them, over.'

46

'Roger. That bloody bulldozer,' Old Norman said, 'over.'

'Roger, anyway we followed the first spoor your game scout showed us. But it went into bad tracking country, very rocky. He was really covering country, thanks to that bulldozer. Anyway we've been tracking him all day. Now we've lost the spoor again in more bad country, and baboon and guinea-fowl have been jumping up and down all over the place. Do you read? Over.'

'Roger, we'll have to do something about that bulldozer, over,' Old Norman said.

'Anything to report? Over.'

'Well, I have been charged by a rhino this afternoon.'

We were all grinning. Old Norman's gentle, matter-of-fact voice:

'I was driving along minding my own business when I saw him in the bush a hundred yards away. So I stopped and got out. I tippy-tippy-toed closer to get a nice look at him, he looked a very nice bull, and suddenly the wind changed and he smelt me and he spun around and took one look at me and charged. Do you read? Over.'

We were all grinning, listening hard.

'Roger, so what did you do? Over.'

'Quick as a bunny I climbed up a tree, over.'

We were all laughing.

'And? Over.'

'He charged my tree. He knocked it about a bit. Huffed and puffed a bit, then he pushed off. Then I pushed off. He was a hang of a lovely bull.' Old Norman said, 'over.'

We were all laughing.

'Which way did he head?' Thompson said, 'over.'

'He set off in your general direction, north-east, over.'

'Okay, we'll keep a look out for him. We'll have to head your way soon. Anything else? Over.'

'Just bring me a rhino, over.'

'Roger-Roger,' Thompson said, 'just grab the next one by his tail, and hang on tight and call us on the Roger-Roger. Four-one, mobile closing down now, over and out.'

He switched off the machine, sweating, red-tanned, blue-eyed, good-looking, baby-faced. 'I wish I'd seen him up that tree.' He unscrewed the aerial, relieved that Roger-Roger would now take his sweating self elsewhere. 'All right,' he said, 'puma. Thank you.'

Roger-Roger clambered up, sweating.

'And,' Thompson said, 'what's your name?'

'Rojah-Rojah,' Roger-Roger said.

'No man, your real name.'

'Sixpence,' said Roger-Roger.

'Sixpence,' said Thompson, 'your best friends will never tell you this, but as I am never likely to be your best friend I will ask you to do me a favour: have a wash tonight. Please, truly.'

'Jebo, Nkosi,' Roger-Roger beamed.

All the Natives laughed.

'Because if you smell like that again tomorrow I shall also be forced to climb a tree in my great fear.'

The natives thought that was wonderful, black, sweating, hung-over faces, grinning white-toothed. Roger-Roger plodded away with the roger-roger on his back and sank down gratefully on his stomach and closed his eyes.

I called the water-man. He was leaning back against a rock with his eyes closed. He got up heavily and plodded over to me with the wet canvas water-bag and handed it to me. I pulled out the cork and drank. I took long mouthfuls, trying to hold the water in my mouth but involuntarily it went down, good and cool and tasting of canvas. It tasted of the many times I had drunk, hot and sweating, from a canvas bag in the bush. It tasted of Africa. 'Thank you,' I passed the bag back to Gunga Din and he passed the bag to Richard and he drank.

'Kalashaka,' Thompson said. Kalashaka opened his eyes and

48

got up and came plodding over to Thompson. 'Vegetation,' Thompson said.

Kalashaka got the notebook and pen out of his pocket and passed them to Thompson. He pulled a handful of twigs out of his pocket. They were samples of bushes that rhino had fed off and it was Kalashaka's job to count the number of times, on any given bush, that rhinos had pulled off a mouthful, to determine their feeding habits. Kalashaka held out the twigs one at a time and Thompson wrote down their botanical names and Kalashaka said: six, fourteen, nine . . . I wondered how Kalashaka remembered, especially today. My guess was that Kalashaka did not remember, he just made up figures to keep Thompson happy.

Thompson did not look happy. We all sat. The porters had their eyes closed.

'Right,' Thompson said, 'let's go and help Ben.'

The sun was going. There was another hour of light at the most. Ben had found the spoor, leading out of the yesterday, today and tomorrow place. We followed it into the sun, spread out, losing it, finding it. Thompson ranged wide, looking urgently; if he did not make contact within half an hour it would be too late. A whole day wasted. It was still bad country, up and down, and rocks, the spoor came and went. 'Come on, madodas, *find* it.' The spoor went over a big hill and then down steep rocks, then into a ravine. Up out of the ravine and up a steep slope and over the top and suddenly Ben shot out his arm and signalled us to stop, flapping his hand, and pointed: and there he was. *Diceros bicornis bicornis Linsaeus*, the armed rhinoceros. As tall as a man, two thousand pounds and armed to kill.

He was seventy-five yards away, across a ravine. He had heard something of us but he could not smell or see us. He was alert, head up, long tubular ears flicking in all directions. He turned with a bustle and looked and flicked his ears angrily and then bustled again. Thompson was signalling for the dart-gun and the gun-bearer was coming crouching. The porters were tip-toeing for the trees behind us, each man claiming his tree. Only another half-hour of light left. Thompson tugged a loaded dart out of his hat, rammed it into the breach. Then he put a slugless cartridge into the adaptor and then rammed the adaptor into the breach behind the dart. Richard was also loading his dart-gun excitedly. Nevin was positioning himself to cover Thompson with the .458, an unenviable job, you got the impression that if anybody shot a rhino to save Thompson's life Thompson would murder him. Thompson crept forward with his dart-gun. Down the slope into the ravine, using the cover of the bushes and grass, crouched, watching where he put his feet. We were dead quiet, still, watching. Each man near his tree.

The rhino stood, alert, ears going. He snorted and turned round angrily and glared. He knew something was up, he didn't know what. Thompson stopped, thrust his hand in his pocket and pulled out his ash-bag to test the wind. He shook the small bag and the little puff of ash sifted through the air and drifted sideways to Thompson. Away from the rhino. Good. Thompson had good cover. We could see them both. Breathless, watching, dead still.

Thompson crept deeper down the ravine. He was sixty yards from the beast now, across the ravine. Still too long a shot for the dart-gun. The beast snorted and spun around and glared, head up, ears going. He had heard something. Thompson froze. The rhino glared, then spun around with another snort and looked in the opposite direction. Thompson shook the ash-bag again. Silver ash floating out in the late afternoon golden sunshine shining through the trees. It floated in a different direction, closer to the rhino.

The damned wind had changed. Dangerously close to the animal, now. It only had to change a little more and he would smell us. I was cursing inside my head. Thompson stood, frozen. The rhino snorted and spun around, ears forward, horn up, took five angry paces towards him, looking for something to kill. Thompson stood frozen.

Don't anybody dare move.

The rhino glared angrily at Thompson's cover, then spun around and glared in the opposite direction. I breathed out. Thompson still stood frozen. Then flicked the ash-bag once. The wind was better. Ideally, in better country, Thompson should have, would have, changed direction. Gone down more with the wind, away from the beast, then stalked back upwind. But this was a ravine, the light was going in minutes. He had to get a dart in soon and the wind could do any bloody thing, or there would not be enough light to track it. Thompson crept further down the ravine.

He was maybe fifty yards off the animal now. To get much closer he would have to go down to the bottom of the ravine and up the other side. That would give him no cover. No decent tree to climb when the beast charged. That would be all right for Coetsee if he were here, Paul Coetsee would tiptoe right up the other side of the ravine and then run right out of the cover right at the startled beast and fire in a dart at fifteen paces and then side-step the furious charge, but then Paul Coetsee was legend, crazy. One of the best hunters in Africa, but crazy, or fearless, or the most unorthodox, or however you describe a man who charges a rhino with a mere dart-gun, instead of the other way round. Thompson was also a very good hunter, but he was orthodox. He had been charged by too many rhinos not to have the greatest respect for them. A rhino will kill you in one terrible charge, throw you thirty feet through the air on top of a thorntree with your guts hanging down to the ground. Thompson was fifty yards off the beast across the ravine, just within reliable range of the dart-gun. I thought: he must shoot now. If he can get a clear shot through all that tangled cover. Thompson raised the gun to his shoulder. I felt good. The rhino spun round with a snort and glared at Thompson's cover.

Thompson froze, gun up. The beast stood, vicious head up,

ears forward. Thompson held the gun on him. But did not fire. He did not have clear vision. Any twig, any flick of grass would deflect the heavy dart. And the beast would be gone. Charge or run, he would be gone. And the whole day gone. He held the stance while the beast glared at his cover, and I imagined I could see his muscles begin to tremble. And the rhino snorted and spun sideways.

The rhino spun, head up, horn up, ears forward at something, spun and presented his whole great flank for target. Thompson hurried three steps down the ravine to get clear vision through the cover, gun up at his shoulder breathless, he got his vision, and the beast heard him and spun back furious to face him, it lowered its head to kill anything in sight that moved, and Thompson fired.

He fired, a crack of gunpowder and the big dart flash. Flashed across the ravine quicker than the eye could see and everybody tensed to scramble up their trees, flashed faster than the furious beast could react, and smacked into the ground five yards short. *Short! The bloody dart had fallen short! bad gunpowder! after all this, after walking all day and hung-over trackers and yesterday, today and tomorrow and the bloody light going and the bloody dart falls short!* I could almost hear Thompson swearing. And *that rhino did nothing.* It spun around with a furious snort looking for something to kill, snorting, ears going. *But he did not run.* Didn't charge, didn't run, just stood there snorting furiously, looking for something to kill, please please please don't run just let Thompson reload his gun please God – Thompson was tugging another dart out of his cap and reloading and I could almost hear him cursing the cartridge manufacturers, the dart, the rhino, the light, the trackers, please please please God don't run just let me load – the rhino spun around again and dropped his head, ears going, snorting, furious. Thompson got the gun reloaded and raised it to his shoulder and the beast was glaring dead at his cover, and

Thomson fired, and there was the crack of the gunpowder. And the bloody dart fell short again.

A big snorting whirl of murder, the rhino whirled furious snorting head down vicious looking for the thing to kill. *And he still did not run, oh thank you God*. Whirled and snorted and threw his great head and snorted and kicked up the dust murder in his heart *but thank God did not run*. Only God knew why this rhino did not run or charge but just huffed and puffed there hating the world, bursting to kill, any second he could change his mind and run and a whole day wasted thanks to the unmentionable cartridge manufacturers, just please don't run just stay for pity's sake huffing and puffing, give poor sweating cursing Thompson another chance to reload his rifle – Thompson was reloading furiously, cursing, only one dart left, red-faced angry khaki in the last golden shadowed sunshine, reloading, *if this bloody one doesn't work*, he raised the rifle furiously and the beast was spinning round furious to face him and Thompson aimed, *please God this time*, aimed high up on the beast's furious head in case it was another dud, and he fired. And the dart flew.

Flew true as an arrow and hit him slap in the middle of the forehead. And there was the magnificent smack of the detonator in the dart as it hit and squirted the M99 deep smack bang into him, and he gave his great snort of fury and charged.

He came charging, crashing, so you could feel the earth shake, making great furious puffing snorts, great black one-ton killer beast as tall as a man with long killer horn, head up, ears forward, he charged down into the ravine out of sight but the sound of his charge was loud and clear, he came crashing huge and terrible up our side of the ravine past Thompson's cover up towards us and we were scrambling flat out for our trees. Scrambled, clutching, clawing up our trees, it doesn't matter if you tear your nails off gouge your eyes out just please God get me up this tree that beast's coming thundering, snorting, hell-bent, one-ton big black killer murderous red-eyed, crashing up at us with the silver dart flashing in the middle of his murderous head, furious for somebody to kill and he saw us scrambling for our trees and it appears that *I me personally myself out of all those present am precisely the bastard he's been looking for all this time to kill* and he gave a great, furious snort of rage and his pig eyes rolled furious red and his great horned head went murderously bullneck down and he swung thundering, snorting on my tree as I scrambled higher, he swung his great head and crashed his horn into my tree-trunk and the tree shook and I clung tight, and he thundered furiously on. Head up, looking for anybody else to kill through the trees festooned with trackers and porters clinging, he swung at another tree with his horn and the tree shook and the African clung on for dear life, and the rhino thundered on. He charged on out of our trees and up the slope and he went crashing out of sight.

We climbed down out of our trees and we were all grinning wanting to laugh and congratulate each other and say it was a beautiful rhino, God, what about those two dud cartridges in a row, two in a bloody row, and why didn't he run after the first dud, God, we were lucky but wasn't he a beautiful rhino? Thompson called for the radio and Roger-Roger came over grinning and Thompson called up Old Norman and told him we had a dart in and that we were about to start tracking him and Old Norman was delighted.

There was only half an hour of light left.

CHAPTER FOUR

THE drug would take about twenty minutes to pull him down. In that time he could be two, three, four miles away, more. The light was going fast. We tracked over the hill, Ben and Nyambi and Thompson in the lead. At first it was easy tracking; then down into another ravine and across and up the other side and then we hit bad tracking country again, and went through old spoor again, and we lost it.

'Find it,' Thompson said urgently, '*find* it!'

We were all spread out looking, every man who thought he knew anything about tracking.

'*Find* it!'

Ben found it; he slapped his hip and we turned and hurried after him. We followed it down the rocky hill, across the dry river-bed, up a long straggling hill through thick bush and over the top, and we had covered two miles. The light was going badly. The trackers were having a hard time following it again. We should be finding sign of his dizziness now, broken bushes he bumped into and places where he had fallen down, but we were not. I thought we were following the wrong rhino. Our rhino must be down now, somewhere in this thick bush country not far away, but we only had about another ten minutes in which to find him. In ten minutes it would be too dark to find him, and he would lie unconscious for the next five hours then come round and stagger off, and we would have to hunt him all over again, or the lions would get him while he was down.

'Hurry!' But the trackers could only work so fast.

When we were almost past him, Richard saw him in the sundown. Off to the side, he was still standing, almost out on his feet, head down. Richard slapped his hip and pointed.

There he was. Big and black and prehistoric, down there among the golden mauving grass. We could only see the top of his back and lowered head over the grass. He looked wonderful. We had worked very hard for him and very nearly lost him and now there he was.

'*Tambo!*' Thompson whispered. He grabbed the ropes and waved everybody to stay well back, and he set off quietly down the hill.

The beast was not yet unconscious. He was still dangerous. He could still make a last drunken charge and spread Thompson's intestines on the treetops. The wind was in Thompson's favour, the sunset breeze quite strong. Thompson crept quickly down the hill through the grass with the ropes. We crouched on top of a big rock and watched it.

I saw the tips of its ears flick once, then its head came up. Thompson paused. He was twenty paces behind the beast. He had the ropes ready in his hands. Then he took another two paces and the beast swung round on him.

It swung round on him with a huge, startled, furious snort gathering itself, outraged, and a calf scrambled up beside it *it was the wrong bloody rhino* and Thompson scrambled. He turned and fled shouting, '*Wrong rhino!*' and we were already jumping up to scramble for our trees. Everybody scrambling all over the place and Thompson charging back up shouting, '*Wrong rhino!*' and behind him the outraged rhino made one token charge after Thompson's disappearing buttocks, then swung aside and went thundering down the hill making her great puffing noises to get her calf away from the danger. We were all laughing. Thompson kept running back up the slope.

'*Find it*,' he was shouting, '*find that spoor!*' He had forgotten the cow and calf.

The trackers were running back up to the place they had left the spoor. When they got there they couldn't find it again in the bad light. We were all looking everywhere.

'*Find it*,' Thompson sweated. '*Please find it.*'

The sun was down amongst the trees on the horizon, flaming red and orange. There were maybe five minutes of light left.

When there was no more light, when the sun was already gone over the horizon and the sky was just flaming red and the trees were mauve silhouettes aflame on their edges and down in the valleys it was deep mauve; when we could track no more, Ben saw him. He was at the far top of the hill, on a pile of great rocks, silhouetted, his great head and horn against the sunset.

We ran up the hill, stumbling in the dark.

CHAPTER FIVE

TWENTY yards off we could hear him, his deep, long, strained unconscious breathing. There he was, collapsed on his great chest and belly right on the top of a steep mass of rocks. His great legs buckled out under him and his head was hanging down. We clambered up the rocks to him, cautiously. He was out, all right. There he was.

He was beautiful, the sunset red-mauve-gold on him, his great, collapsed, sweating body mauve and red and the folds of his hide jet black; and the sunset was on his long, curved horn, and shining in his eyes. His eyes were open, unconscious, glazed, the sunset even on his eyelashes, black-golden, and on the tufts of hair on the tips of his ears, and on the big silver dart with the red, white and blue feathers and on the big trickle of blood running down his prehistoric face.

'Isn't he something?' Thompson's good-looking baby-face was flushed happy in the sunset.

'He's bloody marvellous,' I said.

The natives were clambering all over the rocks saying, *ah! ah!* and staring at him. They lived in the Ruya but it was the first time they had seen a live chipimbiri this close. A man must run from chipimbiri. Ben sat down on a rock with his back to everybody without a shadow of expression on his face. And lit his pipe.

'Roger-Roger,' Thompson said. He sat down on the rock next to the beast's head and patted it once while Roger-Roger came and sat down in front of him presenting the radio on his back. Thompson was happy. He took up the transmitter. 'Four-one, four-one, four-one, four-one, four-one, mobile, over.'

Old Norman's voice came back: 'Roger, reading you strength three, over.'

'Roger,' Thompson said happily. 'Well, we've got him, over.'

'That's *marvellous*,' Old Norman said.

You could hear Old Norman grinning somewhere twenty miles away over those hills and valleys. 'Where are you? Over.'

This was the part that always got me. 'Norman,' Thompson said slowly, happily, looking into the sunset, 'I guess we're somewhere south-east of you—' He looked back over his shoulder to see if he could see any landmarks, any decent hills in the dark, and couldn't, so he looked up at the sky: 'I haven't got a map, got yours handy? Over.'

'Roger, over,' Old Norman said.

Thompson took a breath. 'I'm not very familiar with that map,' he said, 'over.'

'Roger,' Old Norman said, unalarmed.

'But the place where we darted the rhino would be about a quarter of a mile west of a dry river-bed which takes a big loop. I guess it must be the Mudzi river, do you see it? Over.'

I was very impressed with Thompson. How had he remembered that? Today was his first day in the Ruya country.

Old Norman consulted his map. 'The river which takes a big loop is the Bungwe, not the Mudzi, over.'

'Very well, the Bungwe. Well, when we darted him he ran

58

away about south-east from that point, can you roger that? Over.'

'Roger.' Old Norman traced his finger over the map.

'He ran about five hundred yards over the hill in that direction, then he swung away to the south-west. Roger that, over.'

'Roger,' Old Norman said, 'over.'

'He kept going more or less straight south-west for about a mile, then he crossed another river-bed, over.'

'Roger,' Old Norman said.

'Okay. Then he swung right over for maybe a mile, say due south-west, over.'

'Roger,' Old Norman said.

'Then over one, two, three hills,' Thompson counted, 'heading more or less due west, into the sunset, maybe another three-quarters of a mile. And that's where we are. At the top of the third hill. Got that? Over.'

'Roger, I got you,' Old Norman said, 'I'll be there as fast as I can, over.'

'Roger to you and over and out,' Thompson said happily.

I liked to listen to them giving directions. I never knew how they did it. And even assuming navigational genius, Old Norman still had to find a way for the Land-Rover and the Mercedes over those hills and ravines and river-beds and bush, in the dark. It was very impressive, each time. Thompson gave the great unconscious beast a satisfied pat. There was a big groove round his neck, an old snare scar.

'Hullo, beast. You're going to live happily ever after.'

The native porters were still staring and saying *ah* and grinning. They seemed to have got over their hang-overs. Maybe they had not believed that we would really catch a chipimbiri. The beast was still sweating, mauve and black in the late sunset and making his long wheezing breaths. He was hot, under stress from the drug, fighting it. His hide was warm and sweaty and rough and huge-feeling. Thompson had told two porters to build a big fire to the side of the rocks, and the yellow flames leapt up, crackling, from the dry logs and the light danced yellow on the great, black beast and made flickering shadows, and it danced on the shining black faces and on the rocks and the bush.

'Turn him on his side,' Thompson said, 'it's bad for him to take all his weight on his chest.'

They lashed a rope around his jawbone and half-hitched it tight round his horn. They lashed two ropes to his hind and forefeet. Two men held each rope. Half a dozen men crouched down round his belly, ready to shove when the rope men heaved. The yellow firelight flickered, gold and black.

'Be quick to jump if he kicks!'

'Malunga – tshey – tshey – *hiyea*!' Thompson chanted, and they came in in deep sweat chorus: '*HI-YEA!*' and men on the ropes heaved and the others shoved on his great flank with all their might and the great beast rocked on his belly with a huge wheezing moan; he was heaved half-way over, great, roped legs looming up in the fire-light, and then he convulsed. Suddenly he lashed out with a big, protesting, wailing grunt, and bucked his great spine and lurched up his great, drunken head, eyes wild in the firelight, and lashed out his legs, trying to get up, and the natives scrambled and fell over each other to get out of the way and everybody was shouting, *watch out*! Then he crashed back on to his stomach with a great thump, and his head lurched down and he passed out again. He gave a big groaning snore.

We collected ourselves.

'Futi,' Thompson said: Again. He put an extra man on each rope.

'Malungo – tshey – tshey—' and the big chorus, '*HI-YEA!*' and we heaved with all our might, ready to leap out of the way, and the great body rolled three-quarters over before he came round and convulsed, and he crashed all the way over on to his

60

side with a great, twisting thump before he could fight back; he gave one drunken, Herculean thrash, then he passed out again. He lay there on his side in the leaping firelight with his head hanging down over the rocks, groaning.

'Give him a pillow,' Thompson said. He picked up a large flat rock and shoved it on the ground under the beast's head. 'Another one.'

Kalashaka brought another rock and placed it on top of Thompson's.

Thompson locked his arms under the great beast's head and heaved it up with a grunt and Kalashaka shoved another rock on top of the pile and Thompson lowered the head. Now the head was level with the rest of the body. Thompson pulled off his cap and stuffed it under the head to protect its eye. The rhino gave a great long groaning sigh. He was fast asleep again.

We stood back and looked at him. Huge and prehistoric and sweating, fast asleep, snoring on top of the African rocks in the firelight. And the big dart in the middle of his forehead. We were very pleased with him.

Thompson gripped on the dart and pulled. It refused to come out. He got a better grip and twisted it and pulled, like a man pulling a tough cork out of a bottle, and it came out with a jerk. He examined the big bloody needle, as thick and as long as a three-inch nail, and it was twisted and broken. That was why it had been so hard to pull out. It must have hit his skull and bent. There was still an inch of needle buried in his head. The blood was oozing out of the hole, down his head.

Thompson got out his penknife, crouched down and held the knife like a dagger and sunk it slowly down into the small bloody hole in the head, until he reached the skull. Then he waggled it carefully, probing for the broken needle. The beast gave a big long, groaning breath, Thompson crouched ready to jump. But he was fast asleep. Thompson probed around with the knife blade, bloody in the firelight, but he could not find the broken piece of needle. He withdrew the knife and sank another incision, across the wound at right angles.

'I can feel it.' We were all watching. I did not like the look of him probing in the wound, but the rhino was fast asleep. Thompson knew what he was doing. He waggled the knife, but he couldn't get leverage on the needle. He stood up and wiped the blood off the knife on his trousers.

'We'll have to wait till Norman comes and get a pair of long-nosed pliers out of his toolbox.'

I was glad he stopped probing. The animal was not feeling anything, but it did not look good. The forehead is where they take all their punishment when they fight each other, anyway.

'Muti,' Thompson said: Medicine.

The muti-man came with the wooden box. All the natives crowded round. It was a small box full of little bottles of drugs and M99 for the darts and a snakebite kit and some Elastoplast. Thompson picked up a little plastic syringe of penicillin. He snapped the tip off the needle, buried it deep into the bleeding hole in the rhino's forehead. The thick white antibiotic was forced down into the wound and then welled up over the sides thickly, and ran in a long red-white trickle down his forehead. He gave a big groaning sigh. We were all satisfied.

Thompson handed Kalashaka a thermometer and said, 'Take his heat.' Thompson and Richard began measuring him up and Nevin was writing it down on the data sheet.

'Length overall from base of tail to top of lip?' Nevin quoted from the sheet.

'Ten feet, four inches.'

'Height at shoulder?'

They measured him. 'Five feet, six inches.'

'Girth at chest?'

'Eight feet, seven inches.'

'Diameter of foot?'

'Ten inches.'

'Length of horn?'

'Two feet, five inches.'

'Circumference of horn at base?'

'Two feet, four inches.'

'Heart-beat?'

Thompson plugged a doctor's stethoscope into his ears. He crouched down at the beast's roped legs and held the stethoscope against the great chest. He moved the stethoscope about, listening for the best place. Then counted off on his watch.

'Sixteen,' he said.

'Breathing rate?'

I had been counting, my hand against his big nostril. 'Seven per minute,' I said. His nostrils were warm and soft.

'Temperature?'

Kalashaka was holding the thermometer in the beast's anus. He pulled it out gratefully and handed it to Thompson to read. Thompson held it up to the firelight.

'Hundred and two. He's a bit hot.'

The beast was still sweating, in stress under the drug, but he was all right; he was deep asleep. We were well satisfied. There was nothing left to do, just wait for Old Norman to find us.

I lit a cigarette. Everybody was starting to sit down. It was my first cigarette for about four hours and it tasted very good. We had not eaten all day, except for the glucose sweets, and I was not hungry. The cigarette tasted very good going deep down into my system. I sat down and I could smell my own sweat and I felt the good bush tiredness, the third, maybe the fourth time I had sat down all day, and it felt very good. And the big fire leaping yellow and the big red glow of the big logs and the big crackling and the sparks flying up into the starlight like the devil's spawn and the big flickering yellow gold-black shadows in the bush and on the rocks and on the black faces, and there was our great beast, huge animal lying flat out, great ribs flickering gold-black and his great feet lashed up with rope and his huge head flat out fast asleep, flickering, so fast asleep and harmless in the firelight, and the great big groaning sighs, all ours, lying there, and I was happy. I put my hand on his big muzzle again, to pet him, and smoked my cigarette. His big prehensile mouth was open and his big triangular muzzle was soft, I liked to feel it, and his big nostrils breathed long, warm, wet, groaning breaths on my hand and his horn shone sweetly harmless in the firelight, and the good tiredness right down to my bones, and the cigarette, and I was completely happy.

That is how we were sitting when suddenly the beast came round. Suddenly, momentarily, he built up enough oxygen to fight the drug, and his great chest swelled as he sucked in a long, groaning breath and his glazed eyes opened wide and simultaneously his head heaved up, and Thompson shouted, '*Watch out!*' and we scattered. Richard was sitting at the beast's haunches and he leapt off wildly on to the rocks below; the great head swung drunkenly sideways up and his spine bucked and his legs thrashed to get up and his eyes rolled wild and he gave a groaning wail and he got half-way on to his struggling legs and he crashed. We stood scattered, helplessly gaping; in one mighty heave he was thrashing up again wild-eyed in the firelight, he heaved himself up on to his hobbled legs for a long, struggling moment, then he lost balance and crashed backwards on to his haunches, and he threw his head furiously and his forelegs came up, flailing grotesquely in the firelight as if he were doing a trick. Then he went over backwards over the edge of the rock towards Richard standing down there gaping and Thompson screamed, '*Watch out!*' and Richard scrambled backwards down the rocks and fell. The beast crashed down five feet with a thudding grunt on to his spine, his legs thrashing in the firelight, Richard was scrambling up wildly three feet below him and Thompson was screaming, '*Get out the way!*' and the beast crashed down over straight at him. Rolled, huge, grotesque, down the rocks straight at Richard, scrambling for his life, Richard flung himself wildly sideways and there was nothing in the world but the great body and legs and horn crashing down and Richard's long body flinging

64

wildly out of the way and Thompson screaming, '*Get out the way!*' and then there was Richard sprawled out on the rocks, scrambling wildly up again, and the great beast was crashing down past him, on to its crumpled knees. It gave a roaring wail and fought back up on to its legs then crashed over again, down the sloping rocks, into a big boulder which rolled down, and big slabs of rock went sliding after it and the rhino crashed down after them. Then for another long moment he was poised on the rocks, bucking and twisting on his spine then he rolled again. He crashed over against a pile of boulders, and gave one heaving groan, and he went back to sleep.

We were scrambling down the rocks after him. '*Are you all right?*' Thompson shouted to Richard.

'*Hellsteeth!*' Richard said. '*Hellsteeth!*' He was grazed on his hands and knees, and dishevelled and grinning.

'*You were lucky—*'

We clambered down to the rhino. There were broken rocks and scores of his hide. He was flat out on his side; he had exhausted his build-up of oxygen by his exertions and was fast asleep again. The natives stood well back, laughing and *ah*-ing. We kept out of range of his head, in case he woke up again. He was in big leaping shadows down here. Thompson called for light and Ben went up to the fire and brought back a piece of burning timber. He held the flame over the big, crashed beast and Thompson examined him.

He had a big bleeding graze on each cheek, near the eye, and some along his spine and a big one on his side, rough and bleeding, like a pomegranate broken open. His horn was scored. He was sweating and you could smell him very strongly, and he was making slow, groaning noises. Thompson held the burning torch so he could see into the beast's loins to see if there was any injury to his genitals. There was the big sack; it was very dirty and sweaty and there were engorged ticks embedded in the folds.

'Family jewels okay.'

He pulled off a big engorged tick and put his boot on it and it went pop and blood squirted dark red on the rock.

'He's all right.'

He looked up at Richard.

'And you?'

'I'm all right,' Richard grinned. He had been very lucky.

'Take his heart-rate then please.'

Richard fetched the stethoscope. Thompson asked me to count the beast's breathing and told Kalashaka to take his temperature again. I put my hand over his warm, soft, wet muzzle and looked at my watch, keeping well out of range of his horn. Thompson ordered that he be roped down to the ground. They tied a rope tight around his jaw and horn and another round his hind-legs and they led the ropes off to two different trees and lashed him down. We reported his heart-rate, breathing rate and temperature. He was all right. Fast asleep.

We stood around and looked down at him.

'Isn't he something?' said Thompson.

'But you were very very lucky, my boy.'

CHAPTER SIX

WE heard Old Norman's vehicles before we could see them, a faraway grinding that came and went in the hills. We had been waiting nearly three hours. The drug would only work on the animal another two hours. Then he would wake up properly and all hell would break loose.

'Isn't that a good sound?'

It was a very good sound indeed. We were pretty tired and hungry now. We had smoked nearly all the cigarettes. Most of the hung-over natives were asleep round the fire. Ben just sat there, smoking his pipe, staring into the fire. It seemed that he had not moved once. Ben was from across the border in Botswana, and I think he was half Bushman, although he denied it. All other tribes think that the Bushmen are only animals.

'Kunjani, Ben?' Thompson said to his back.

'I am well,' Ben said very quietly, without moving his head.

'You did good work today,' Thompson said.

Ben didn't move. Ben knew he had done good work, hangover or not; it had been very bad tracking country.

We saw the headlights of the vehicles, maybe two miles away. They were coming grinding, *bundu*-bashing, over a ridge, the lights glowing in the bush, grinding and going from side to side, looking for a way, first the Land-Rover, then the Mercedes. They could see the glow of our fire easily now, and they were beaming in on it. But there were still all kinds of ravines and river-beds between them and us. The lights went out of sight down beyond the hill. We sat there waiting for them for a long time and the sound disappeared. Then we saw the lights again and they were beaming up the last long hill where we had lost the spoor in the dusk and seen the cow and calf, shining up into the night like searchlights, and we could hear the engines grinding and the thuds and bangs. Then the headlamps came over the hill, first the Land-Rover's, then the great Mercedes's, and we could see the gang of Old Norman's Africans walking ahead with the axes and picks, the vehicles grinding after them. You could hear the bangs and thuds of the rocks hitting the axles and undercarriages and crushing the bushes over, and the Africans shouting. Then they stopped. There was a belt of trees and rocks there was no way round. More shouting, and then the sound of the Africans chopping down trees and the sound of the picks on the rocks. Then the engines grinding again.

Then they were clear of the bad trees and they came down

the rest of the steep hill and then up through the trees to our big rock hilltop with their glaring headlights.

Old Norman climbed out of his old Land-Rover and came climbing up the rocks to admire the rhino in the firelight. 'Very good,' Old Norman said to nobody. 'He's a hang of a nice bull.'

Nobody congratulated Old Norman on finding us. I always thought it was very impressive.

Mkondo was reversing the Mercedes round so that the rear pointed uphill towards the rhino and Thompson was supervising some natives clearing some of the trees and rocks. The big rhino sleigh was lashed to a winch on the back of the lorry. The rhino was still quite high up on the big rocks, but he had saved us a lot of trouble by falling as far as he had. The natives lowered the back flaps of the lorry and dragged off the runners for the sleigh. The runners were fourteen feet long and made of heavy steel and it took ten men to handle each one. They dragged them off and hooked them on to the back of the lorry to form a ramp for the sleigh, like a railway track. Thompson climbed up into the cab and worked the tipping mechanism and there was the whir of the big hydraulic tip and the back of the lorry began to tip up in the firelight. When it was fully tipped, so that the back of the lorry and the steel runners made a straight incline down to the ground, Thompson worked the winch and the rhino sleigh began to slide, scraping slowly down on the winch cable and grinding down the runners, and down to the ground, flat. We were all gathered round it, to lug it.

It was fourteen feet long by seven feet wide, made of stout timber bolted to a steel frame and it was very heavy. We crouched down, thirty men round the edges, and got a grip on it and there was the big *HI-YEA!* and we heaved the sleigh up and staggered with it towards the rocks. We got it to the beginning of the rocks and we thumped it down. Then we got another grip on it and chanted again and we started lugging it, stumbling up the big rocks. We dragged and shoved and

68

dragged and shoved it over the rocks, a yard, a foot, a few inches at a time scraping and heaving and shoving it, panting, stumbling, cursing. We got it up the rocks and crashed it down beside the rhino and rubbed our aching hands. We were all breathing hard and smelling of sweat. The next trick was to get him on to the sleigh.

The beast lay on his side, his spine against the edge of the sleigh. We lashed two ropes to his feet again, and another rope round his throat and horn. Eight men on each rope, half a dozen to heave on his stomach. Two ropes were lashed to the two big ring bolts on the top end of the sleigh. Six men held each rope to stop it sliding back down the rocks. If he woke up again on this slope there would be a mess. We braced ourselves.

'Heave,' Thompson said and we heaved. The men on the leg ropes heaved and the men on the stomach shoved and the men on the sleigh ropes took the strain with all their might, everybody heaving and shoving and straining in the leaping firelight on the big, sloping rocks, and the great bulk shifted and his roped legs began to loom up in the air, up, up, up, unconscious body being manhandled over on his spine and he emitted one long waking groan of protest. 'Heave!' Thompson shouted, 'heave! heave!' and we heaved and he was half-way over, giant legs up in the air and he started to thrash. 'Heave!' Thompson bellowed and he flung his shoulder against the beast's bucking side and everybody heaved with all their might, and the beast really woke up, he thrashed and bucked and the sleigh skidded and jerked and everybody was straining – Heave! and the great legs and bucking body crashed right over on to the sleigh. He thrashed and the sleigh skidded and jerked and everybody hung on with all their might, sleigh, rhino and half of us could go crashing down the rocks. 'Hold him down!' Thompson bellowed and he threw himself on the animal's flank with all his weight and hung on him, 'Hold him!' he roared and Ben jumped on to the sleigh and threw his weight on the beast, and Nevin and Kalashaka and Richard, khaki and black and white

69

and sweat and teeth bared, grunting, shouting, hanging on arms and legs and shoulders and the great black rope-entangled beast thrashed underneath them and the Africans strained on the ropes with all their might. Then he gave a great groaning snore and went limp, back to sleep.

They climbed off him slowly, releasing their weight one at a time, panting. He was fast asleep again.

They lashed his great head and chest down on to the sleigh, to ringbolts. Ben dragged the winch cable up to the sleigh and hooked it on to the ringbolt. Thompson put another rope and three men on to the ringbolts at the upper end of the sleigh. Then he sent Nevin down to the Mercedes to drag in on the winch.

'Right,' Thompson said. 'Poly-poly.'

There was a whir and the winch took up the slack on the long cable slowly, then it took the strain and the big sleigh with its great animal jerked on the big sloping rocks and the men on the other end took the strain on the ropes to brake it. '*Poly-poly!*' Thompson shouted, and the sleigh slid grinding and jerking and creaking down the sloping rocks with a scraping noise, dragged down by the winch and braked by the sweating men on the ropes, jolting and creaking and scraping all the way down to the bottom. And the smell of sweat.

Then thirty men pushed, and the winch dragged the big sleigh over the rough, stony ground, up to the ramps, and with thirty men shoving and chanting and sweating the winch dragged the sleigh up the ramps and up on to the back of the tip lorry, screeching on the steel, and the great beast slept through it all.

CHAPTER SEVEN

WE rode jolting on the back of the Mercedes, Old Norman leading the way on the trail he had blazed in to find us. Jolting, banging, grinding through the bush, shouting *Bossopo* and ducking for the overhead branches, hanging on cold and happy because we were going back to camp, the natives in a very good mood, singing *We have captured a great chipimbiri* and joking and shouting *Bossopo* when the overhead branches came, and the great beast lying there fast asleep in the midst of us, lashed down, jolting and bouncing fast asleep on the first leg of his long journey to a new country far away where no man would kill him; lashed down there, with his big prehensile mouth that he chomps up whole thorn branches with hanging open, making his great long, groaning, complaining breaths, his vicious horn stretched out harmless and his glazed eye half open and the trickle of dried blood and penicillin across his great head and Richard sitting astride his shoulder hanging on to the head rope so it didn't work loose. Over the ridges and down and around the ravines swinging round the trees and rocks and grinding down over the steep banks into the riverbeds and changing to four-wheel drive, the great diesel raced and roared across the river-bed so the cold sand flew, and ground up the other side: for one hour it was like this, and it was nearly ten o'clock and the moon was well up, shining silver on the vast silent bush bouncing past and on us and on the great rhino lying stretched out there, when we saw the fire of Old Norman's camp ahead on the banks of the Ruya, and we knew we were half-way home. On the other side of Old Norman's camp we came upon the native kraals again; they came running out of their kraals in the cold moonlight to see us, the big lorry and the men who were rumoured to be catching chipimbri, shouting and clapping their hands in glee and the children dancing up and down and shouting to us to stop so they could see the chipimbiri and our natives on the lorry shouted, *'Chipimbiri – Chipimbiri – we have here a live chipimbiri!'* and laughed, feeling very superior to be those who captured chipimbiri, and we all laughed. Then we came to the track that the bulldozer had cut, a wide, dirt swathe through the bush and we were only half an hour from home and our dust rose in a great silver cloud behind us.

The Mercedes was doing thirty miles an hour down the dirt track when I felt the beast's green vomit on my hand and I heard the big strangled belch and his great head lurched frantically. I shouted, *'Watch out!'* and he convulsed with a great vomiting belch, wide-eyed, desperate for air through the vomit in his windpipe, and threw all his frantic strength into the great lurch of his head, fighting for his life for air before he drowned in his own vomit; in one Herculean thrash he snapped the big rope on his head and his great horn swept across the sleigh and he bellowed and everybody scrambled, shouting, and Richard clung astride his bucking shoulders to the broken rope shouting to Mkondo to stop and the giant hobbled legs flailed wildly, and collected Roger-Roger smack in the chest and he gave a thumped shout and disappeared over the side of the lorry into the clouds of silver dust at thirty miles an hour, and the rhino was fighting wildly for air, and Thompson's head stuck out the cab window shouting, *'What's wrong?'* and then Mkondo slammed on the brakes and the lorry skidded to a halt. Thompson leapt out of the cab before the lorry was stopped and ran back down the road to Roger-Roger and the rhino was still crashing and fighting for air.

'Are you all right?' He grabbed his arm.

'Jebo.' Roger-Roger was rubbing his head, dust everywhere and the rhino was still crashing.

'Did you fall on your head?'

'Jebo, Nkosi.'

He was all right.

'Then you must be all right.' Thompson ran for the lorry and vaulted up on to it. The rhino gave a big thrash and retch and the vomit spewed out of his mouth and nostrils, and his windpipe was clear. He lay panting exhausted in his green vomit, his heart thumping and he gave a big, gurgling groan and went back to sleep.

'His heart's hammering,' Richard said, 'I can feel it through his shoulders—'

Thompson grabbed the muti-box and snatched out a syringe of nalorphine, antidote to the M99. He had to have the antidote in case the M99 made him vomit again and he drowned. Thompson grabbed the rhino's ear feverishly and pinched up a vein. He jabbed the slender needle into the tough skin and the needle bent and the vein slid out of the pinch and Thompson cursed. He pricked and jabbed again and he got the vein and he pumped the antidote into the beast's ear, then he rubbed his hand roughly over the beast's eye to make it wake.

'*Go!*' he shouted at Mkondo, '*go like hell!*'

The Mercedes revved and lurched and roared off down the track crazily as fast as Mkondo could drive her and we lashed the beast down again with every piece of rope we could find.

He was coming round as the Mercedes roared jolting into our camp, half-drugged spasms jerking against the ropes in his old vomit and big protesting groans, and then his eyes glazed over again, regathering strength, then another spasm. Mkondo swung the Mercedes round the stockade as the beast gave another great kick, then braked and reversed the big lorry up to the stockade. The two game scouts were clambering up the stockade to open it. The rhino gave another lurch.

'*Kowleza – kowleza!*'

The game scouts were on top of the stockade feverishly hauling up the vertical mopani poles hand over hand, throwing them clear to the side with a crash. *'Quickly before he comes right round!'* Thompson went into the stockade, shouting to them to hurry. The poles were heavy, you could see the game scouts sweating in the moonlight. *'Come on, come on, madodas!'*

Mkondo reversed the Mercedes into the entrance as the game scouts were heaving the last poles out. The rhino was coming round fast, lunging against the sleigh ropes. The labourers were dragging the big steel runners off the back, shouting, they man-handled them into position and already Richard was working the tip mechanism and the back of the lorry and the sleigh and the rhino were looming up into the moonlight, and the rhino gave a big wailing groan at being tipped up and he thrashed and the sleigh rocked. Thompson shouted, *'Let him come!'* and the sleigh came screeching down on to the runners and the rhino gave a big thrash as the sleigh hit the ground, then a big groan and his eyes glazed again.

'Untie him off the sleigh.'

They undid the knots across his head and chest carefully, expecting him to thrash as soon as he felt the pressure go. The knots parted. The beast just lay there, his feet still hobbled. Groaning. We all stood well back.

'Humba, Mkondo!'

The lorry dragged the big sleigh out from under the beast. We stood well back ready to scramble. He gave a groan as he woke under the movement, he slid off the sleigh to the ground with a thump that made him belch and he gave a big thrash against the ropes and we jerked, ready to scramble. Then he just lay there and his eyes glazed over and he groaned.

'Close the wall!'

The labourers were passing the big poles back up to the game scouts and they were ramming them down back into the gap. Thompson was filling the penicillin syringe, then filling another syringe with the other half of the required antidote, the nalorphine. *'Kowleza, kowleza madodas!'* There were only a few gaps left. He pulled out his penknife.

'Light.'

A game scout clambered along the top of the stockade with a lantern and held it so it shone on the beast's head.

'Sit on him, madodas.'

They got down on him gingerly, six grown men, all over the animal wherever there was space on him to hang to, and hung on.

'Hold tight.'

Thompson gripped an ear and started sawing into the tough gristle with the penknife to earmark him and we all held tight for the beast to thrash, for the ear is the most sensitive part. He twitched his ear and gave a big sigh and snored. Thompson sawed as fast as he could, teeth clenched, and his hands and the knife gleamed sheeny red in the lamplight. He cut out a triangular wedge of ear two inches long, then tossed the piece of ear into the night. They hung on tight and he grabbed the other ear and started to saw rapidly, and the big ear twitched back flat on his head and he gave a big waking groan and Thompson sawed hard and they pressed all their weight down, panting. The blood was a shiny red pool in the dirt in the yellow lamplight. Thompson tossed the other wedge of ear out over the stockade.

'Poor old bastard.'

He unscrewed the needle off the penicillin syringe, held the needle like a dagger and slapped it into the rump, it went home and the beast gave a lurch and they pressed down on him with all their might; Thompson screwed the syringe back on and pumped thick penicillin into the beast.

'Other one.'

The game scout passed him the syringe of antidote.

The beast's eyes were suddenly wide open and he groaned once loud and bucked and twisted his back and thrashed his great hobbled legs and the men lunged all their weight down on him and his big, rough body twisted underneath them; they hung on and he bucked and twisted, then he groaned and went limp.

Thompson slapped the needle into the hide and shot the antidote into him. Then he ran to the stockade wall and passed up the syringes. He hurried back to the beast's hobbled legs. He knelt and loosened the first slip knot, so it was just finger tight, watching the beast all the time and the men hung on. Then he loosened the second and last slip knot. Now he only had to pull on the rope and the slip knot would spring open and all the ropes would be loose. The beast lay there panting.

'Right,' Thompson whispered. 'Get up slowly. One at a time. And get the hell out of here.'

They got up off the great bulk, one at a time, and tiptoed away. The beast didn't move.

'Get out, get out.'

They clambered up the mopani log walls, up on to the top of the stockade and stood there. The beast lay there groaning.

Thompson crouched by the legs impatiently until they were all out. Then he gently pulled the slipknot out. The knot came apart. The animal did not move. If he got up now he would tangle himself up in the loose ropes for a while. Thompson was ready to jump, he gently, ever so gently, began to disentangle the loops of rope off the forefeet. We were all watching.

He eased the ropes off, watching. The rhino gave a big groan, and just lay there. Then he turned to the hind-legs, and he tugged gently on the loops, and the animal thrashed. It gave a groan and its eyes rolled red and it convulsed its head and haunches like fish flapping and the legs lashed out, and Thompson scattered back kicking up dust and the animal swung up after him. After him, as quick as a flash it bucked up on to its forefeet and the blood flew from its angry cut ears and Thompson made for the wall with the bleeding beast two yards behind him, it swung round with a great lunge, scrambling on to its hind legs with a snort, it lunged one yard after him furiously,

76

bloody-faced, and its legs buckled under it and it crashed. Crashed on to its chin and over on to its shoulder and Thompson was reaching at the wall, the beast scrambled back to its feet with a furious stagger after him, vicious horn, wild-eyed, murder-bent, snorting to kill, and its drunken hindlegs buckled and it crashed over with a great thud of dust and Thompson scrambled up the wall to the top. The natives were shouting and laughing with glee. The beast made a try to scramble up again, and fell the other way with a groan in the dust; it lashed its legs once, and then lay still; it swelled up its great flanks in the lamplight and its eyes glazed over. It had exhausted its oxygen.

We lined the jagged top of the stockade and looked at it lying flat out down there, dazed dirty bloody in the lamplight. His ears looked very sore, the two big wedges cut out of them bleeding vermilion into the dust in the lamplight. In a minute he would come round again. He lay there, groaning deep.

'*Hey!*' Thompson shouted. '*Wake up!*'

The sore ears twitched once.

'*Aaarh – Oi!*' Thompson screamed at him to get through to his dazed brain, '*Wake up!*'

The ears twitched again, bloody.

'*Oi – aarh!*'

No response.

'Everybody scream,' Thompson said.

We shouted and screamed abuse and exhortations at the tops of our voices in English and vernacular, and he did not move. was deep asleep again.

'Bring a bucket of water.'

Thompson perched up on top of the stockade, and tossed the bucketful of water out into the pen. It landed with a splash on the beast's head and shoulders and kicked up dust. There was a stunned second's silence, then the great beast reacted to the shock. He groaned and clambered drunkenly to his feet. He looked around drunkenly wet for somebody to kill, then just stood there, dripping water and blood.

'That's my boy,' Thompson said, very pleased.

The beast took a few staggering paces then stopped, looking round groggily in the yellow glare of the lanterns. Then he swung around ponderously and lumbered a few steps in the opposite direction, then stopped. He flicked his bleeding ears back and forth, then held them back against his head. He could hear us standing above him, lining the top of the stockade, but he could not yet make us out because of the glare of the lamps. The water had dissolved some of the congealed blood on his ears and face and it dripped. He heard somebody up above and he spun around very quickly and took two thundering paces, looking, then stopped when he could see nothing to kill. He swayed once, then he saw a tangle of rope in the dust, something foreign, and he gave a great snort of rage and dropped his bloody head, his eyes rolled red into the front corners, and he thundered head down at the rope and tossed it so it flew up in a big tangle across his horn. He gave another angry snort, swiped his horn again to kill it dead. The rope landed back draped around his horn and he lost interest in it. He stood there panting, blinking bloody in the lamplight with the rope festooned about his horn. He was still groggy.

'Hey,' Thompson said, 'go and drink!'

The beast spun on his direction in the lamplight and charged the stockade wall, red-eyed, great feet thudding, and crashed into the mopani logs and the whole stockade shook; he got his horn between two poles and snorted furiously and lunged his great neck and wrenched his horn out and lunged again, swiping and goring the pole. Then he backed off and stood there panting and blinking. He had not seen the water yet.

Thompson climbed down off the stockade and walked round to the corner where the water-hole was. He pushed a stick between the poles into the pool of water and splashed it around. The beast turned furiously on the sound and charged into the pool of water and crashed the corner poles with his horn murderously. He smashed the poles around then backed off furiously. Then he noticed his wet forefeet, and the water he had muddied up. He lumbered up to it sniffing and stuck his prehensile mouth into it and slurped.

'*That's* a good chap.'

We were very pleased with him. He drank up a lot of water, then backed off and looked around for something to kill and found nothing. Then he noticed the freshly cut fodder branches hanging from the stockade walls. He lumbered over to one and bit off a branch as thick as a hockey stick and started munching it thoughtfully.

We were very pleased with him.

'Turn off the lamps,' Thompson said.

The lamps were turned off and the bright silver moonlight was left. We stood on the top of the stockade and looked down at our great beast standing there silver in the moonlight with the smell of dust, chomping up his branch, and we loved him.

'Let's go and eat.' Our first meal of the day.

We climbed back off down the stockade and the rhino spat out his branch and snorted and charged, crashing his horn furiously against the poles. He was all right. He charged and thrashed the stockade until we were all off, then he stopped, listening. Then he picked up his branch again and resumed chomping.

As we walked back to our tents we heard the sound of another branch breaking in the moonlight, and new chomping.

Part Two

CHAPTER EIGHT

DOWN in Mususumoya, in the Umfurudzi on the Mazoe River, on the edge of Chief Maramba's country, where Coetsee and Thompson were conducting Operation Rhino together before coming to the Ruya, there are fewer trees, the country is flatter; the dry, yellow elephant grass grows ten, twelve feet high and, usually, when the rhinoceros charges there are no trees nearby to climb, or, if there are, somebody is already clambering up them ahead of you. It was very difficult and dangerous hunting and usually you could not see more than a few paces ahead in the tall elephant grass; sometimes you only saw an ear flick or the tip of a horn sticking up when you are almost on top of him, and sometimes you would not see him at all, only hear him, and sometimes, if you had that ability you could only smell him.

Coetsee could smell them. Paul Coetsee is one of the best hunters in Africa. That is a matter of opinion and that is everybody's opinion. Coetsee does not stalk a rhinoceros and dart it from sixty paces and run for the trees when it charges. Coetsee charges the rhinoceros and darts it from twenty paces, or ten if he can, and when the beast charges he stands still while the others are running for the trees. Coetsee will stalk through the jesse bush so thick that a man can neither aim nor run at all, and poke the dart-gun out with one hand and dart the beast from one pace. It is said Coetsee is fearless. It is said he is crazy. Everybody says Coetsee is going to get himself killed by a rhinoceros.

Some men are born great hunters, some achieve it. With Coetsee it is the first. It is many things. I do not pretend to understand it, any more than I understand what makes a great bullfighter, but it is at least all these things: courage, brain, knowledge, cunning, instinct, stamina, decisiveness, a kind of military genius. With Coetsee it is at least one thing more again. It is telepathy. A tele-imposition of his will and superiority on the beast by concentration, an unfaltering conviction of his own superiority. A lot of people say Coetsee is going to get himself killed by a rhinoceros. Coetsee knows he won't be. A lion maybe, or an elephant maybe, but a rhinoceros will never get him. You ask him how he knows and he says he just knows.

Coetsee went to the soothsayer before Operation Rhino began, because a good soothsayer can also know such things. He told Coetsee many things. He told him that he was a man who worked with wild animals, and that he was about to begin a very dangerous operation to capture a very dangerous kind of beast. He told him that one man would die in a vehicle connected with the operation, and that two other men would be injured by the wild animal, one very seriously. The first man to be injured would be young and tall and dark-haired. He described this man and the description he gave was that of young Richard Peek, precisely. The second man to be injured would have blond hair. Coetsee and Thompson and Nevin are all blond.

At Mususumoya camp, in the Umfurudzi, at the start of Operation Rhino, Coetsee met young Richard Peek for the first time and he recognized him from the soothsayer's description. He took Richard aside and he talked to him very strongly, like a Dutch uncle. He told him that he was going to be very careful indeed: no risks, no heroics, or he was going to kick his arse all the way back to Salisbury. The next week Fosbury was killed.

81

Fosbury was Coetsee's assistant and he killed himself turning over an Operation Rhino Land-Rover.

Then Coetsee told them about the soothsayer. And he told young Richard very strongly again: no risks or he would kick his arse all the way back to Salisbury. That left the blonds. Young Nevin was also advised very strongly that he would also get his arse kicked all the way back to Salisbury if he took any risks. That left Thompson and Coetsee. Thompson did not need any warning. Thompson knew what it was like to be under the thundering hooves of a rhinoceros. He knew as much about rhino as anybody.

That left Coetsee. And Coetsee knew it would not happen to him.

CHAPTER NINE

HOT. It was high noon, when rhino like to lie up in some shade. They came tracking down the long slow slope, Coetsee and Kapesa, Kapesa in front tracking and Coetsee some paces to his side, and Richard behind them with the .458. Some distance behind came the others; it was often hard to keep up with Coetsee, he and Kapesa could work many miles very fast together. In Mususumoya the hunting covered more country, because the rhino were scattered wider apart, and they were getting very wild; they were running great distances when they got wind or sound of man, or even when they just crossed our tracks of yesterday.

The spoor led down the slope into the dry river-bed and up into the tall elephant grass on the other bank, along a rhino trail, a sort of path through the elephant grass, and they stopped. It was very hot in the river-bed, the sun beating up off the sand, and very still. When he got down there in the river-bed Coetsee could smell the beast.

He signalled to the porters to stand still. He tested the wind with his ash-bag. It was in his favour. He signalled to Kapesa and Richard to follow at a distance. Then he went into the elephant grass after the rhino he could smell somewhere in there.

Coetsee stalked silently down the trail, bent, sweating reading the sign, and he was as afraid as the next man. Kapesa and Richard crept, following at twenty paces. They could not see Coetsee ahead of them in the tall grass. Ahead, thirty paces, two trees stood well apart above the tall grass. The rhino probably lay under one of them.

Coetsee crept down the trail. It took a turn in the high grass and then ahead lay an area of sparse grass, forty paces wide, and then the thick grass started again. Just in the thick grass across the open place stood the tree, and under the tree, in a small dustbowl, stood the rhino. He stood with his massive hindquarters into the small hot wind so he could scent what was approaching him from behind and see what was coming from the front, and hear what was coming from all sides. He was dozing, head down in the shade, sideways on to Coetsee, and Coetsee could just see the top ridge of his great back and the tip of his horn through the grass.

Coetsee signalled to Kapesa and Richard to come up, fast and quiet. Then he signalled to Kapesa to go twenty paces through the grass, to the edge of the sparse area. He signalled Richard to stay where he was with the .458. Coetsee pulled out his ash-bag and tested the wind. It still lay as the beast was indicating. Coetsee stared at the beast. Then he left the cover of the elephant grass and he entered the sparse area.

He ran crouched down on tiptoe, expertly silent through the sparse yellow grass in the open, straight at the beast that would kill him with one throw, ran to take the beast by surprise, to have the advantage of initiative, to put it in the position where it had to deploy to his tactics and not vice versa; to force his decision on it, Coetsee ran straight at the beast, crosswind, through the tall sparse grass, ten, fifteen, twenty paces, twenty-five, and the beast heard him and it turned.

It spun around with a huff and a snort, vicious, startled, on guard, as tall as Coetsee and a dozen times as heavy, with deadly armour, whirling round, red-eyed, snorting to kill, and Coetsee stopped dead. He could not get a safe shot through the tall grass, he wanted to get a reliable flank shot and he stopped dead and stared at the animal, panting and sweating. They stared at each other, blue eyes staring out red eyes rolling wild, astonished; Coetsee stood there, crouched, panting, and stared the beast out, and the great beast gave a furious roar and dropped its head wild-eyed and charged. Charged thundering, snorting, great black head down and Coetsee just stood there, crouched, sweating, staring as the beast came charging, it came thundering straight at him, and stopped. It thundered to a halt ten paces from the man and the dust puffed up round its great feet and it snorted, puffing wild-eyed, at the man and it jerked its great head, red-eyed, and Coetsee just stood. Then it backed off to charge again.

It backed off huffing, head down, eyes wild, lumbering backwards through the elephant grass gathering its great armoured bulk to charge again. It lumbered back ten paces and Coetsee just stood there, staring the animal in the eye, concentrating all his will power on it, and the beast snorted once more and then charged. The earth shook, it came thundering through the grass down on Coetsee to kill, and Coetsee stood, and it came thundering, snorting, red-eyed, to a halt again. It stood there, great flanks heaving, glaring, and Coetsee stood crouched, staring at it. He did not raise the gun. The movement would have broken the spell, the something between them, the man imposing his will, his presence, his superiority. That would have been broken and the beast would have charged all the way and Coetsee only had a dart-gun. The rhino stood, huffed and puffed, for five seconds, ten paces off, then it backed off again for the final charge.

Coetsee crouched there willing Kapesa and the beast and himself, waiting for Kapesa to create the diversion so he could get a flank shot. The beast lumbered back snorting through the grass, glaring at Coetsee; it stood one moment, gathering its huge self and then it charged, and Kapesa acted. The beast charged at Coetsee and thirty yards behind Kapesa stepped out of the elephant grass to show himself and clapped his hands once and the beast saw him and swerved to charge Kapesa. It swerved in full charge and thundered headlong at Kapesa and Coetsee pivoted as the two-thousand-pound beast thundered past him five paces away pounding the earth, and he slapped a dart into him. There was a crack of the cartridge in the pounding of the earth and the silver dart with the red, white and blue fletches smacked into the great galloping rump, and Kapesa was running for the tree. He got to it ten paces ahead of the animal, it gave a great toss of its head at the tree trunk, and then it crashed on into the elephant grass, the silver dart flashing in its side, and it disappeared.

Maybe the whole business had taken sixty seconds.

CHAPTER TEN

WHEN the cow was four years old she went on heat for the first time and in her urine there was a hormone which the big bull smelt, and he found her in her territory in the Umfurudzi; she tolerated him in her territory because of her condition and because he was amorous and as persuasive as a rhinoceros can be. She allowed him to mount her, great lovable unlovely lovers. She permitted him to stay with her two days for this purpose, then she would tolerate him no longer and he went away, happily bad-tempered.

One year and five months later the calf was born; and he was thirty inches long and fifteen inches tall and he weighed sixty pounds, and of course he had no horn yet. For three months he suckled and then he began to eat branches, those he could reach, and she pulled branches down for him to get at, and he chomped them up, thorns and all, chomp chomp chomp. But he still suckled as well. He kept suckling even when he was so tall he had to go down on his front knees to get to her teats, even until he had to go down flat on his belly. For eighteen months she suckled him and she roamed far and wide with him every day, to keep him moving so that the lions would find it difficult to get him. She was still suckling him, when he insisted, when she went on heat again and another bull smelt her out and she was tolerant of another rhino again, and she mated again. The calf would have stayed with her for another eighteen months, until the new calf was born, and then he would have given up and left and gone his own way.

The calf was half-grown and his dam was nine months pregnant with the new calf when Operation Rhino came to Mususumoya.

There was a cold sunrise north wind blowing, bending the grass. They stood and examined the spoor that Old Norman's trackers had led them to, and cursed the wind. The spoor was on a soft sand trail through the grass and it was new and clear, an hour or two old, even the wrinkles on the hooves showed up; but it was going to be no good to them, because of the wind. A man only had to kneel down and blow on it and the spoor would be disguised, one breath and it would look like yesterday's spoor. And the spoor went in the same direction as the wind, as they knew it would, for the rhino would like to go with the wind, the better to scent what was coming behind. It had been the same yesterday. They had followed a spoor so fresh that it

86

was almost impertinent, they followed it with the wind and all the way the sign was fresh, no more than half an hour old, dung that was still wet warm and pad wrinkles still clear, but it was no good. The rhino went with the wind and the wind carried their scent to him and he kept moving. He had kept moving till sundown and they had to give up. Today it was going to be the same. So they set off into the wind, spread out wide, looking for other spoor in the rough grass country. At noon Ben found it, the spoor of the cow and calf. They followed it till one o'clock, when they found them lying up in the shade, and Thompson got a dart into the cow, and she scrambled up puffing and snorting and furious and she ran with her calf, and the calf galloped behind her, ears back.

The big pregnant cow ran, the silver dart flashing in her flank, making snorting, huffing noises to warn her enemy wherever it might be and to keep her calf by her, and her calf galloped behind her. She ran out of the grassland and up the rugged hill as fast as she could to put as much distance between the enemy and her calf, and the calf galloped flat out behind her, ears back. She ran over the hill and down the other side into a ravine and across the dry river and up into the rough hilly country, and she was beginning to sweat. She slowed down to a great heavy trot, big hooves pounding the earth like a cart-horse, head and horn up, alert ears forward, looking from side to side as she trotted, her big pregnant belly jerking. For fifteen minutes she ran like this, through three miles of rough hilly country, and she began to feel the effect of the M99.

She was sweating heavily now, a black sheen of sweat on her back and neck and belly and between her legs, and her heart was pounding and she was panting and she began to feel dizzy and her breathing began to labour, and then she began to stagger. She shook her great head to clear the dizziness and her mouth and nostrils were straining wide open and she was making sucking noises. Now she began to feel the drag in her legs and she began to stumble and buckle and she lurched and

87

her great head jerked down and she was groaning. She lurched against a tree and tore the bark off, she blundered on right through a bush and trampled it flat, blazing a big blundering trail for the trackers to follow. The calf trotted behind her making miaowing noises. She lurched into her calf and knocked him over and he squealed, she lurched straight into a tree head on and she fell right over with a great grunting crash on to her chest with her massive hindquarters stuck up in the air, and then she crashed over on to her side. The crash woke her up momentarily and her eyes rolled drunkenly wild, and she clambered back to her feet, blundered on up the hill, wheezing, and the calf kept himself behind her out of the way.

At the top of the hill was a steep cliff, maybe fifty feet high, with big rocky ledges at intervals. The big cow staggered on up the long, rugged slope, stumbling and lurching and crashing against trees and trampling over bushes and overturning stones, her heart pounding and her hide shining in sweat. She was forty yards from the top of the cliff now, and the calf followed her. She staggered on up the hill, trying to get away from the drug, and she lurched from side to side, staggering and bumping against trees and crashing on to her knees and groaning, wheezing, struggling back up again to her buckling legs, and she was twenty paces from the clifftop now and in another two minutes she would be unconscious. She got to ten paces from the clifftop and she hit into a tree and she fell.

She crashed on to her side and lay there groaning and the calf stood beside her whimpering and twitching his ears and looking all about; then the big cow got up again. She clambered up and staggered towards the clifftop, she got within three paces of the clifftop then she lurched to the right. She stumbled along the top of the cliff, head down and eyes dazed and legs buckling, for twenty paces, groaning and then she veered right away from it, and the calf trotted after her, whimpering. She banged into a tree and nearly fell over, and she lurched and turned towards the clifftop. She staggered forward, ten paces,

88

nine, eight, seven, six; she stumbled on a stone and nearly fell over, then she righted herself and she stumbled on right to the edge of the cliff, and the calf followed her; her big heart was pounding and she was covered in sweat and in a minute she would collapse, and she staggered right over the clifftop.

She fell forefeet and great head first and she gave a wild screaming groan, she fell twelve feet screaming and crashed on to the first big ledge, and her great hindquarters came over and she rolled, falling great legs everywhere great belly crashing down the steep cliffside, rolling over and over banging and crashing, she crashed on to the next ledge and her great weight kept her rolling, and the rocks thundered down after her and the stones leapt over her, and the dust. She fell all the way down the steep sides to the bottom and then crashed to a stop on her side, and the rocks clattered down about her.

The calf stood on the top of the cliff horrified and panic-stricken, and he made to jump over the edge after her, then his fear stopped him. He scrambled backwards, panic-stricken without his mother and whimpered and ran along the clifftop, heart thudding, then he tried to jump over again, but he could not bring himself to jump and he jerked back. He ran back whimpering to where his mother had gone over and he stuck his head over the edge, ears forward, looking for her and he tensed himself to jump and crouched down, but he could not bring himself to do it. He pulled back horrified at the height and his heart pounding and he ran along the clifftop desperately look-ing over for a place to go down, where he could slide down on his hooves or even a place to jump that was not so high, he ran all the way to the end of the clifftop and he could find no way down and he did not know what to do. He turned and ran back looking over the edge for a way down, milling around and look-ing panic-stricken and trying to make himself jump, he ran on along the clifftop, stumbling and looking over the edge and his panic getting bigger and bigger all the way, he ran right to the end of the clifftop, and then there before him he found a way down. It was very steep and rocky but it was not a cliff any more and he crouched down and launched himself over, and he went crashing down the steep rocky slope, slipping and sliding and skidding and grunting, hooves out, head down, rump up, scrambling and skidding and falling over and scrambling up and sliding and dislodging all kinds of rocks, all the way to the bottom. And he came to the place where she had landed, and she was not there.

Maybe it was the great shock of the big long fall, or the pain in her great belly, or maybe it was that she had not felt much because she was drugged, but the big pregnant cow had first lain there on her side groaning, and then she had got her breath back and she had got back to her feet. She had staggered up, groaning winded, sweating, with the blood running from the big bruised grazes, and she had walked a quarter of a mile from the cliff, and then she had collapsed. She struggled grunting and groaning back to her feet and she blundered her head and shoulders between two big boulders, and she passed out. She went to sleep on her feet, with great long groaning breathing, and she was still on her feet fast asleep when the calf found her.

He went galloping up to her panting and whimpering and trembling, and he nudged her in the belly with his head and short horn, nudged her again, then he went round the other side of her making his relieved panting miaowing noises and he nudged her on the other side. Then he stamped his feet. He milled around a long time. He looked all around with his ears going in all directions, then he went back to her and decided to have a drink. He got down on his knees, and then flat on his belly and got hold of one teat and he started sucking. He was not very thirsty but it was something to do. He sucked noisily for five minutes, nudging up with his head to get a better grip on the teat with his big mouth, then when he had had enough of that he got up and milled about a bit. Then he lay down, since his dam had taken it into her head to go to sleep.

The trackers saw where the tracks led over the cliff and they were very alarmed. They found the way down the steep slope. When they found the cow the calf was suckling on the other teat.

They wanted to get the cow back to the camp as quickly as possible and if they were to dart the calf he might run a long way before he fell. They decided to try to catch the calf by hand. They spread out quickly and quietly and began to close in. When they were forty yards off the calf smelt them.

He scrambled up from under his mother's belly and looked wildly in all directions, ears cocked, and he saw them and gave a terrified snort of warning and he turned to his dam. He turned to alert her to protect him, he gave her a big nudge in the rump with his stump horn, then he swung back to face the line of men. They advanced on him, and they were pretty nervous themselves. The calf snorted and ran round to the other side of his mother and then turned to face the men and he dropped his head and then jerked it up at them and snorted to terrify them, and they still came. He ran round to the other side of his mother and he backed up against her snorting and feinting with his horn, but they were still coming. Then he lowered his head and he opened his mouth and roared and he charged, but it was only a feint; he charged ten paces thunderously then he skidded to a stop and he backed up to his dam again hurriedly. The line of men was twenty paces off now. He snorted and roared and charged again head down, came thundering down on the near-est men and the men broke and ran and the calf spun around and went galloping back to his dam, then spun around to face the men again, panting and trembling and wild-eyed. When the men were fifteen paces off Coetsee and Thompson came forward out of the line and advanced on him.

They advanced from two directions, each holding a big hank of rope, and the calf huffed and puffed and snorted and tossed his head trying to look in both directions at once. He feinted with his horn in both directions, he charged two snorting paces head down at Thompson then he scuttled back and looked wildly, then he charged two snorting paces at Coetsee, back-scuttled to his dam and then both men lunged at him with the ropes. Coetsee ran at him from one direction and Thompson from the other and the calf gave a squeak-snort of terror and rage and he charged Thompson.

He charged, head down, hooves pounding, and Thompson stood his ground with his rope to tackle him, ready to dodge, the calf charged helter-skelter terrified snorting and Thompson began to dodge and the calf swerved and hit him. He hit Thompson smack bang full tilt on his thigh with his stump horn and seven hundred pounds and Thompson flew, arms and legs flailing, backwards with a thump on the rough ground, and the calf charged after him furiously and hit him again with all his might on the buttocks and Thompson rolled over and over down the slope, and the little rhino charged after him, head down, and thumped him again. He thumped Thompson flat out in the hip and Thompson rolled, bruised dusty cursing arms and legs everywhere, then he scrambled up, sweating dusty bruised bleeding cursing, and he scrambled for his dart-gun. The little rhino was charging round in a swoop to get back to his dam and Thompson flung up the gun and smacked a dart into his galloping rump and he gave a squeal of terror and he swung aside and fled, flat out, into the bush. Thompson sent trackers running straight after him, rubbing his bruises and cursing and got straight on to the roger-roger to call Old Norman to come and fetch them.

The calf ran for two miles. When they caught up with him he was staggering round in circles. They roped him up tight and administered the antidote right away. It took a lot of men to hold him down.

CHAPTER ELEVEN

IT was dark when they got the pregnant cow and the calf back to the stockade at Mususumoya. They put the calf into a pen adjoining his mother's in case he bruised her more, and left him tied up while they attended to the cow. She was bruised and had big grazes, but otherwise she seemed normal. She was still deep asleep, taking the long groaning breaths, which was also normal. But they were very worried about her pregnancy. They gave her the penicillin and the antidote and untied her legs, and they got up on top of the stockade to watch her come round, anxiously. She looked very bruised and swollen and pregnant lying in the dust. They called to her to make her wake up, then they shouted at her, but they did not throw water on her for fear of the shock. It took her a longer time than usual to wake up, and her getting up was very ponderous and staggering, and she fell over a few times before she steadied up, and the falls worried them too, because of the pregnancy. She staggered round the pen bumping and buckling and she looked very miserable and she went back to sleep a few times, wheezing on her feet, and they shouted at her to make her wake up and to take a drink of water. They stuck a stick between the poles and they splashed the water around to make her see it. There was an adult rhino bull in the next pen and he huffed and puffed around the pen, backing off and then charging at the mopani poles, snorting so the dust flew up, trying to get at the cow to kill her, then glaring through the poles at her, then backing off again and then charging again. The cow took no notice of him, she just staggered and bumped around her pen and then she started calling her calf and the calf, lying all trussed up in the next pen, answered her. But they did not want to untie him and distract her with him until she had taken a drink. They kept splashing the water and calling to her, to wake her up properly and to get her mind off the calf, and she staggered and bumbled around the pen a long time, and then she found the water and she drank.

Then they untied the calf. Four men sat on him to hold him down whilst his legs were untied, and then they scattered. The calf scrambled to his feet and charged after them scrambling out of his pen, then he heard and smelt and saw his dam through the gaps between the mopani poles. He ran and pressed his nose against the poles and miaowed to his dam. And the cow came staggering up and pressed her nose against the poles and miaowed to him, comforting him. After a long time she woke up properly, and they stood nose to nose at the mopani poles whimpering to each other. The men went to bed, still very worried about the pregnant cow's bruises, but relieved that she was looking better. The cow and the calf called to each other all night.

The pregnant cow fed quite well and she watered well, but she was very listless. She just stood around in her pen head down a little and sometimes she lay down. She did not huff and puff and snort at the other rhinos nor at the men who came to the stockade to worry about her, she just stood there, and she called to her calf a lot, standing with her nose against the poles. At eight o'clock on the third night the big cow aborted.

The game scout came running to Old Norman's tent to tell him that the cow was aborting and Old Norman ran to the stockade, and there she was.

She was standing with her head down and her nose against the poles close to her calf and she was groaning, and the blood was running thick and shining red out of her distended vagina and down her massive hind-legs, and there was a big pool of blood soaking into the dust. In the middle of the big dirty pool of blood lay the foetus. It was eighteen inches long and twelve

94

inches at the shoulder and it was black and shiny and soft-looking, and it was perfect, and you could see it was a little bull foetus. It was perfectly formed already; its very small eye was closed, and the small ribs showed softly against the satiny hide and the three toenails on the small hooves were transparent-looking and its soft ears were folded back wet and shiny sleek against its head, and the wrinkles in its hide were very soft, and its hide was shiny yellow-black-red with blood in the lamp-light. It was dead. And on the other side of the poles the half-grown calf stood with his nose against the poles right close to his mother's nostrils.

There was nothing Old Norman could do. He tried to climb down into the pen quietly behind her, to examine her, to see if there was anything he could do, or if he could drag the foetus away from her, but when he got half-way down the stockade she heard him and she turned on him, sick and staggering and bloody and furious, and Old Norman had to scramble up. She would not let him into the pen and she certainly would not let him pull the foetus away from her. When she had chased Old Norman away she stood glowering, and then her head lowered, sick, and she put her big nose down to the foetus lying there and she smelt it, then she turned around ponderously in the muddy blood and she put her nose back against the mopani poles sep-arating her from her calf and she made miaowing noises to him and he answered.

There was nothing Old Norman could do. Except shoot another dart into her to put her to sleep for a few hours, but the shock of that might kill her. Old Norman got on to the roger-roger and radioed Salisbury for a vet to come, but it would take a long time for the vet to get out to Mususumoya. There was nothing Old Norman or anybody could do. He climbed back on top of the stockade with his lamp to sit the night out with her.

She stood there with her nose against the poles whimpering to her calf and the blood ran hard down her great legs in the yellow lamplight. There was much blood in the pen now, nearly the whole pen was under dark, muddy blood. At midnight she collapsed. She staggered and drooped and at last collapsed on her great side in her blood, with her muzzle still against the mopani poles, and she lay like that, groaning and whimpering to her calf. She was bleeding badly to death. There was nothing Old Norman could do to help her. She lay there with her nose against the poles whimpering to her calf and dying and on the other side of the poles the calf lay down also to get close to his dam, and he miaowed to her. He could smell her blood. They lay like that all through the night and she bled all the time. She died before dawn, and her pen was a quagmire of muddy blood now in Old Norman's lamplight, and when she stopped breathing the calf began to whimper very hard, he lay flat out on the ground with his nose pressed against the mopani poles and cried loudly.

In the first light Old Norman got the Land-Rover up to the pens and he lashed ropes to the dead cow and the foetus and he dragged them away. When he dragged her away the calf set up a great commotion and he darted up and down the wall of his pen. Old Norman ordered the labourers to shovel all the bloody mud out of the pens. He dragged the carcases two miles away through the bush, so the calf could not smell her, and then he cut her open and did a post mortem. She was only badly bruised inside from her fall. Then he built a great fire and burnt her.

The natives wanted to eat her, but Old Norman said No.

They stayed two months at Mususumoya and they captured seventeen rhino and translocated them to the Gona-re-Zhou. At the end there were still four rhino left in the Umfurudzi, possibly six, but they had become very wild. They were running thirty and forty miles in a day to elude the hunters. At the end of two months they moved camp to the Ruya, up in Chief Masoso's country. They would come back another time to Mususumoya, after the Ruya. Then they would go to Gokwe.

1. A drugged beast is being offloaded from the back of the Mercedes recovery vehicle into the stockade at Nyamasota.

2. Released from the stockade at Chipinda Pools, Gona-re-Zhou. It has lost its front horn in its attacks on the poles of the stockade.

3. A calf is being lassoed in the stockade at Nyamasota.

4. Suckling. The cow stands about five foot, six inches at the shoulder. Note her newly-made earmarks.

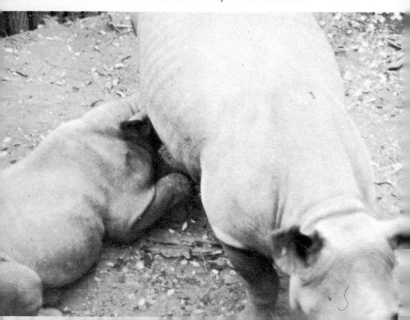

5. A beast unconscious at the end of a hunt. It is being measured.

6. An African game scout examines a fallen beast; the author looks on. Photograph by Thompson.

7. A darted beast has tripped over a tree trunk, semi-conscious, on to its knees. Thompson is roping its hind-legs.

8. The same beast, not yet unconscious, has managed to get back to its feet and is leaning groggily against the tree trunk and the ropes binding its hind-legs.

9. A small calf, legs roped, is being held down while Thompson measures its foot.

10. An unconscious beast is being heaved on to the sleigh, for loading on to the recovery vehicle.

11. This beast clambered up a great pile of rocks before collapsing. To get the beast off the rocks, on to the sleigh, will take a great deal of sweat.

12. A fallen beast has been rolled over on to its side to take its weight off its chest. Richard Peek is taking its heart-rate with a stethoscope.

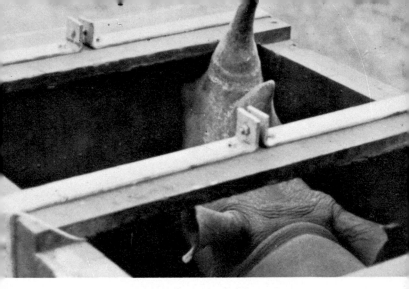

13. This rhino has been crated at the stockade at Nyamasota preparatory to its journey to Gona-re-Zhou.

14. A rhinoceros, called Barbara, in the process of trying to attack the beast in the adjoining pen, right.

15. Another beast collapsed over highly inconvenient rocks.

16. An unconscious beast has been covered in evergreen leaves to shade it pending the arrival of the recovery vehicle.

17. A rhino has just been successfully crated at Nyamasota.

18. The hunting party tracking up a dry river-bed in the Ruya.

19. A beast is being goaded with sacks to charge out of its pen and through the gap into the passage which leads to the crates.

20. The same beast charges through the gap at the sack.

21. A beast is being heaved on to the sleigh. It has woken up under
the manhandling and is lashing out with its horn.

22. A cow has been darted, and has fallen, and now her calf has
also been darted at the place where she fell.

Photograph by Thompson.

23. This drugged beast, whilst still hobbled, has revived unexpectedl in the stockade.

24. The same beast has collapsed again. The beast will now be earmarked and treated, then the antidote will be given.

25. Coetsee, left, and Thompson are trying to catch a calf with ropes to avoid darting it. Photograph by Rhodesia Information Department.

26. A drugged beast staggers up before its legs have been roped. Thompson and Coetsee leap on to it to pull it down. Photograph by Rhodesia Information Department.

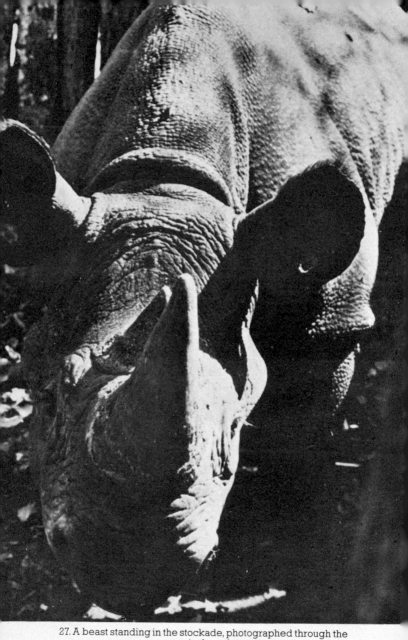

27. A beast standing in the stockade, photographed through the gaps in the poles.

28. Coetsee tests the wind with an ash-bag.

29. A beast revives suddenly in the stockade; Coetsee leaps for safety. Note its angry eyes.

30. A beast being released at Gona-re-Zhou.

Part Three

CHAPTER TWELVE

At first, in the Ruya, it was very good. Every day we got a rhino. Every day before first light Old Norman sent his game scouts out from his camp on the banks of the Ruya, every day with the sunrise they came running back to his camp with information of spoor and Old Norman got on the roger-roger and called up Nyamasota, *Four-one, four-one, four-one, four-one,* and then Thompson's voice bawled out in the cold early golden morning, *Chi-pim-biiiii-ri!* and we scrambled, came running out of our tents still pulling on our clothes, and me shouting back at Brightspark Tafurandika to bring me an orange and a mug of coffee and a handful of glucose sweets up to the Mercedes. Mkondo always had the Mercedes ready and he always looked wide-awake and somewhat aloof, like Ben, and he always smelt of toothpaste first thing in the morning. Mkondo had his own old brass bedstead and his own tarpaulin spread under a mopani tree well apart from the other Africans, including the game scouts, and his blankets were always neatly folded on his brass bed. The game scouts had their own camps, tidy with Government issue, and the locally-hired natives slept wherever they liked, with their own blankets beside their fires, and they looked very scruffy and tattered and unreliable beside the neat khaki-clad game scouts with their dark-green kepis; but even the locally-hired natives looked pretty good next to my old Brightspark Tafurandika who came panting through the long, early-morning grass slopping my mug of coffee in one hand and my handful of glucose sweets in the other and my orange tucked under his toothless chin, very glad to see the back of me for the day. All Brightspark Tafurandika's clothes were old, but the clothes he wore in the bush were very old indeed and consisted almost entirely of ventilation. It would have been no good trying to tart Brightspark Tafurandika up in a uniform. You could not have got over that very bad face, and he would have flogged the uniform at the next beerdrink and come back to camp naked and complaining loudly of robbers. He would even exhort you to call the police, from Salisbury. As God would have been his witness. In that first week at Ruya I never had a chance to take more than a few mouthfuls of Brightspark Tafurandika's coffee before everybody was assembled at the Mercedes and Thompson shouted us aboard and Mkondo roared the big engine and started us bouncing down the long, cold, early-morning tracks to Old Norman's camp. In that first week there was plenty of good spoor and although it was difficult tracking country because of all the rocky hills and ravines and gullies we always made contact by about noon, early afternoon at the latest, and Old Norman came and got us and the beast out and back to Nyamasota usually before midnight. In the first four days we got four good bulls and so our stockade was full of snorting rhino, each in his own pen, who huffed and puffed at us and tried to get at each other through the gaps between the mopani poles, charging each other and crashing their vicious horns into the poles and between the poles so that the stockade shook; and in the night we could hear them standing in the moonlight calling to each other with little high-pitched miaowing noises. They were keeping each other company, complaining to each other. When the pens were full we got them into the big crates, and got the crates on to the lorries, which was a job that took a whole day, and they left in convoy on the seven hundred mile non-stop journey to the vast Gona-re-Zhou. It was a hell of a job getting them into the crates and they kicked and crashed with their hooves and horns, they had not liked the pens and they hated the crates even more, they did not know what a good long life they were going to have down in the Gona-re-Zhou, where no poachers were going to get them. Every one of them had a big, old snare scar round the neck or round the foot, and they were all young animals. We found three skulls of rhino in that first week and we could tell from the teeth that they were all young adult animals.

The skulls were Old Norman's business. Old Norman knew more about catching poachers than anybody. While we were out there catching the rhinos Old Norman was quietly working on catching the poachers. Quiet, soft-spoken, gentle Old Norman loathed poachers. So did the black game scouts who worked for him. The game scouts had good reason. All their lives the game scouts set out on their bush patrols for weeks on end, with a roll of bedding and a pair of handcuffs and a note-book and pencil, and patrolled alone, without even dogs. You cannot take a tracker dog into elephant country for the elephant will chase the dog and the dog will come running back to you with the elephant hot after the dog. They patrol with firearms. And many a game scout has tracked poachers for days and sprung them in their camps and arrested them, and walked them back for days to camp, single-handed. And many of them have been attacked by poachers and left for dead. Smash him, hit him, club him, spear him, shoot him, and when he's down, broken and bloody, hit him and smash him some more and then grab up your gear and run and leave him there to die; leave him for the lions and the hyenas and the soldier ants and the sun; it doesn't matter about him just so long as we get away and can carry on poaching. And a good few have died at the hands of the poachers, shot and axed and clubbed, all alone in the middle of the bush with no one to hear them shout, no one to find them for a very long time, long after the hyenas and vultures. Four of the bastards speared Nasilele to death near Fort Victoria. The bastards shot Magoda through the head at point blank range in Wankie. They clubbed Manjata at Wankie and threw him on the fire, and when he was found the flesh on his face was burned fused with the flesh on his bicep. The wife of one bastard axed Tivana four times in the head from behind in Gona-re-Zhou and then threw burning coals over him before running away. Many spearings and axings and clubbings and shootings, and many many threats. You have to be a vicious, cold-blooded, bad bastard to be a poacher, to man and beast.

Old Norman knew a lot about the poachers in the Ruya long before he got there. He got the information from many places. He knew most of their names and he knew where most of them came from. The trick was to find them and get the evidence, then catch the bastards. But more than them, bigger game than only those who lay a line of snares and long agonized death: Old Norman was after the whole vicious network, the men behind the scenes, the wholesalers, the middlemen in the cities and the men down at the sea, the dealers in large-scale death who commissioned the killing, who bought the hides and the horns and the ivory from the poachers and shipped it out. Old Norman was after those wholesale bastards.

Old Norman and his game scouts worked very quietly and unobtrusively. Let them think I'm stupid, Old Norman said. And he sent his game scouts out in peasant clothes, and planted game scouts amongst his locally-hired labourers, and moved about amongst them speaking only Chilapalapa and pretending he could not speak the real dialect which he understood very well, and pretending to be stupid and quite uninterested in anything other than finding rhino spoor, and he kept his eyes and ears open. And in the night his game scouts came back and told him what they had seen and heard out in the bush and in the labourers' camp and in the kraals, and bespectacled Old Norman pieced it all together and wrote it down, and bided his time and told nobody what he was doing, not even Thompson or Head Office.

CHAPTER THIRTEEN

THE snare was made of high tensile steel cable which the poacher had taken from a mine-dump, and he had heated it in fire to break its springiness and to make it rust, to disguise it. Then he had made a small eye by looping the cable back on itself and bolting it with a small u-bolt, then he threaded the other end through the eye to make a noose. He came to the Ruya from a long way away with a suitcase. It contained many nooses, an axe and an old muzzle-loader rifle, and home-made gunpowder, and a bag of nuts, bolts, ball-bearings and nails as slugs for the muzzle-loader; the snares and the muzzle-loader all had the *mushonga* on them, the *muti* and spell of the witch-doctor he had consulted to give him good fortune. He went deep into the Ruya country, and he built a fence of brushwood half a mile long, and in the fence he left gaps, and in the gaps he hung his neck nooses, anchored to trees.

The young rhino cow sensed the danger when she had her horn and her right forefoot through the noose, she jerked backwards and she got her great head out but she dragged her forefoot, and she pulled the noose tight. She felt the drag and lumbered backwards, snorting, and she wrenched it tighter, she turned to run and the noose tripped her and she fell. She crashed on to her chest and the noose bit through her hide into the flesh. She scrambled up, roaring with fury and shock and pain, and lunged away again and she crashed again. She scrambled up and this time she heaved backwards, and her leg wrenched out in front of her and she fell again. She got up roaring and terrified and wrenching on her leg, she lunged, trying to run, and she turned around and wrenched and reared up, wrenching, and with each wrench the noose cut down deeper. It cut down through her muscles and tendons and still she fought, and the tree to which the snare was anchored shook. She fought for one hour and with each wrench the cable cut deeper, right down to the bone, and then it began to crush into the bone, and then the cable snapped near the pressure point of the eye. The poacher had heated the cable too long in the fire and weakened it, a matter he later noted with irritation, resolving to be more careful about it next time. The cow crashed over when it snapped, then she scrambled up, frantic, and ran hobbling off, but the noose of the cable was still embedded down into the bone. The broken ends of the rusty cable splayed out stiffly into her flesh but the flesh and the u-bolt prevented it from working loose. She ran hobbling and stumbling and lurching on the foreleg with the snare embedded tight into the bone, putting as much distance as she could between herself and the terrible place. She left a long trail of blood and an easy spoor for the poacher to follow, but he did not come back to his snares for two days and he was very annoyed about the broken cable and it was too much trouble to follow her and kill her, and the cow got away. Then the real agony started.

For three months the cow lived with the agony of the rusty cable embedded into her bone, and the great swollen poison, and the stiff broken wire strands splayed out into her flesh grating. Then the big wound began to heal. The poisoned flesh began to grow over the rusty cable and the tendons and the muscles began to grow back together and she could put the forefoot down to hobble on and she learned to live with pain. The hide grew back over the big circular wound, but it did not heal over the place where the stiff wire strands of the broken cable splayed and grated; the wound was always open and suppurating there, and there was a ring of suppurating sores round the foot, and it was swollen, and the poison oozed out.

Then the big bull found her and she mated.

The calf was six weeks old when we got on to her spoor early in the morning. She was limping as she walked but she had control and she had learned to live with the pain. Thompson got a dart into her on the edge of tall grass and she ran hobbling for one mile before she went under, and the calf lay down beside her and suckled. Thompson slapped a quarter of a dose of M99 into the calf and he jumped up and looked around frightened and stinging from the dart. For three minutes he shuffled about anxiously, looking this way and that, ears going in all directions, and we sat sixty yards off and watched him; then he began to go down. He staggered and he began to shuffle in wider circles round his mother, then he wandered off dopily, and we got up and followed, walking with him, to see he came to no harm. He walked groggily, stumbling and breathing hard, and the big dart in his shoulder looked very sore to such a little rhino and he fell into an ant-bear hole, head first with his hind-quarters sticking out. He heaved himself backwards up out of the ant-bear hole and staggered on and Thompson tried to hold him but he was still too strong to hold unless Thompson put all his weight on him. He walked round in a big loop and came staggering back at us, he was very groggy now, and then he passed out. We roped him up well and administered the anti-dote and in three minutes it was taking three natives to hold him down. Then we saw the condition of the cow's foreleg.

That night, back in the stockade, Thompson tried to operate. While she was still asleep under the M99 he cut down into the big open sore, following the cable; then he realized how deep it went. He stitched her up and radioed Salisbury to send a veter-inary surgeon.

CHAPTER FOURTEEN

THE news of the impending operation by the white animal doctor on the sick chipimbiri spread far and wide through the Ruya. Chief Masoso's people came from twenty miles, young men and women and old people and children, walking through the hot, dry bush. They started arriving the next day, before the vet got through in his Land-Rover; they crowded round the pens to peer between the mopani poles at the chipimbiri the crazy white men had captured. I noticed Brightspark Tafurandika moving amongst them with an air of proprietorship and I suspected him of trying to flog them tickets to the show, but he denied it hotly.

'Did you shoot medicine into the small calf too?' Brightspark Tafurandika said to change the subject.

'Yes.'

'Ah!' Brightspark Tafurandika said, 'that was unnecessary. I would have caught the calf with my bare hands.'

'Good,' I said. 'Tomorrow when the doctor operates we must first get the calf and put it in a box and I will tell Nkosi Thompson that you will catch the calf for him with your bare hands and he will be very grateful.'

'Ah.' Brightspark Tafurandika said, 'I would be glad to help Nkosi Thompson but I have responsibilities towards my children.'

I said: 'I will even take a photograph of you catching it with your bare hands. And I will send the photograph to Hollywood.'

'Hollywood-i?' Brightspark Tafurandika said, interested. 'Where is Hollywood-i?'

'Hollywood is in America where they make all the pictures. And all the beautiful girls will see the picture of you catching the chipimbiri with your bare hands and they will say: "*Ah!* – there is-i Brightspark-i!" '

'No,' Brightspark Tafurandika said regretfully, 'I am an old man and I have responsibilities towards my children.'

The next morning they were gathered round the stockade at first light, over a hundred of Chief Masoso's people, waiting for the spectacle to begin. It was a lovely day for an operation on a chipimbiri. Thompson ordered them to climb down off the stockade but he was glad they were there. Let them see the horrors of snaring. A murmur went up as John Condy, the vet, came walking up from his tent with his equipment.

First Thompson climbed up on to the top of the stockade with the dart-gun and shot a large dose of M99 into her. The natives loved that and Thompson had to shout at them to keep quiet, this was a tragic matter they were witnessing, not a circus. The natives all put on solemn faces. We lined the top of the stockade for twenty minutes, waiting for her to go down, and the natives found her very impressive, *Ah! ah!* When she was down we dragged up a crate and opened the stockade. We got a lasso over the calf's head, and dragged him squealing and protesting away from his collapsed mother and into the crate, out of the way, and the natives loved that too, and Thompson had to shout at them again to be quiet, this was a matter for tears not laughter. Then he ordered the labourers on to shovelling all the dung out of the pen. Then John Condy told his assistant to damp the earth down with buckets of water and disinfectants, and the natives thought this was the beginning of the magic, chasing away the evil spirits, and they were very solemn, for evil spirits are no laughing matter at all. Then the cow's hind-legs were roped. Condy sluiced off the festered fore-leg with disinfectant. Then he asked for six labourers to sit on her to hold her down in case she came round, and the natives began to get excited. Then he spread a rubber mat on the floor of the pen and he spread out his surgical instruments and the natives thought it was wonderful.

Condy cut down into the suppurating wound where Thompson had probed, he opened it up wide and deep till all the stiff splayed rusty strands of the broken cable were exposed. And there were her muscles and tendons, swollen and white and yellow and bleeding, and where the wire strands splayed out into the flesh it was grey-green-red, oozing blood and pus. He worked each rusty strand out clear of the flesh with the forceps, then he worked a pair of wire-cutters down as far as he could into the wound and he nipped off the splayed strands, one at a time, and pulled them up out of the way, bloody and covered in pus. It took a long time. Then he cut and probed down the cable as far as he could go. Then he looked up at Thompson. 'It's gone right down *into* the bone,' he said. 'And the bone has grown back over it.'

'*Over* it?'

'The whole noose is covered in new bone. Only this end is sticking out.'

It made me feel sick. The rusty steel cable embedded in the living bone and the splayed ends sticking out and moving with the flesh every time she moved her leg? It made me feel sick in my guts.

'I can chisel it out,' Condy said. 'It will take a long time. It will be a beating for the bone and risking all the muscles and tendons. She will be laid up a long time. How is she going to get around and look after herself and the calf?'

Thompson shook his head.

Condy said, 'Alternatively I can cut out the section of cable still protruding from the bone. That will take the pressure off the leg tissue. Then I will separate the remaining stumps of wire so that they don't rub together in the flesh. Then the wound should heal.'

It made me feel sick.

'What about after-care?' Thompson said.

'You'll be able to move her down to Gona-re-Zhou. But you'll have to keep her penned for a while. And dart her again several times to give her penicillin. And I'll have to come to see her and renew the dressings and take the stitches out.'

Thompson said, 'What about the pain?'

'She's learned to live with the pain. It will be less painful than it was before the operation.'

Thompson straightened up. He was holding a syringe of M99 to give the anaesthetic a booster in case she woke up. He was angry.

'Do what you think best.' He glared at the black faces crowding the stockade, peering through the gaps in the mopani poles at the great beast. '*This*,' Thompson shouted at them holding out his hand at the leg, '*this is what Chief Masoso's people have done! May they be ashamed! This*,' he pointed, '*is why we have come to this place without God!*'

They looked very solemn for Thompson's benefit.

Condy started on the cable protruding out of the bone. Chisel, forceps, wire-cutters, long-nosed pliers, strand by strand he chiselled open the stump of cable and separated the strands, then he dug down into the bloody suppurating wound with the pliers and wire-cutters. Strand by strand he separated, then he manoeuvred the wire-cutters down into the bloody pus-covered flesh as far as he could, then he squeezed the handles and you could hear the *clip* as he nipped the strand through. Then he pulled out the cutters and probed for the piece of wire he had nipped, with the forceps. Between each cutting he swabbed deep into the wound with cotton-wool in forceps and then quickly looked for the next strand to have a go at before the blood seeped back into the hole. Sometimes a piece of bone chipped away when he was working with the chisel and he cursed under his breath and got it out with the forceps. For two hours Condy worked crouched down on the ground and the sun got higher and the heat built up in the pen, and the smell of the earth and the rhinos in the next pens, and the wet herbivorous horsy smell of their dung, and then the sharp smell of the sweat starting on the Africans pressed round the stockade, and our sweat. Condy stopped work to take off his sweater and then he had to stop work more and more frequently to stand up and stretch his aching legs. First the Africans were very interested, then they got restless, then they got bored. From time to time Thompson took her heart-rate with the stethoscope and their interest perked up. Once he took her temperature with the ther-momenter up her anus, and they thought that was excellent. Then, when Condy was very nearly finished with cutting away the wire strands the rhino woke up, and they thought that was wonderful again.

Wonderful, she suddenly gave a big groan and opened her eyes and her legs bent up and she thrashed on the ropes trying to get up and Condy scrambled backwards clutching his instru-ments and everybody scattered back and Thompson screamed, '*Hold her!*' and flung his weight on her haunches and the six Africans threw their weight over her. She wailed and thrashed her legs and threw her head, wild-eyed, and her great body twisted, trying to get up, and Thompson and the Africans hung on shouting and grunting; she tried three times to get up, beat-ing her head against the earth, then she gave a great sigh and went back to sleep.

Condy cut out the last strands and picked out the last chips. Then he swabbed it out the last time. He packed the big wound with antibiotic powder, then he stitched it up with a very big needle. It was hard work pushing it through her hide. He forced through forty stitches of stout gut and carefully tied stout knots and snipped off the ends. The Africans thought the stitches were very good. Then Condy wrapped the wound around with lint, and bound the lint to the leg with white adhesive plaster. He wrapped the adhesive plaster round and round the great foreleg until it was a big, fat, white, nice-looking, secure-look-ing bulge all the way round the wound. And he was finished. And the natives thought the bandage was absolutely splendid, and so did I.

CHAPTER FIFTEEN

In the third week in August it was the beginning of the end of the long, dry winter and suddenly the days were getting hotter, in the middle of the day it was burning hot and there was very little shade under the hard, bare trees. In the afternoons clouds began to come from the north, white at the edges and dark grey in the middle; they were the beginning of the summer rain-clouds, but they would not rain yet, not until October, the suicide month, when the Ruya would be nearly dry and the animals and the cattle very thin. We looked up at the afternoon clouds and wished it would rain. It would have been good if it showered every night to damp down the earth and wash out the old spoor and leave today's spoor fresh. The tracking was getting very difficult. Now the rhino knew they were being hunted and they kept moving big distances and on the hard, dry earth it was often difficult to read the sign, whether it was today's or yesterday's.

Then Thompson sprained his ankle and young Richard had to do the darting, the Richard whom the soothsayer had described to Coetsee. I don't know whether Thompson paid much attention to soothsayers but he said to young Richard what Coetsee had told him, that he would kick his arse all the way back to Salisbury if he took any risks, sprained ankle or no sprained ankle.

'Yes, Ron,' young Richard said, he was very keen. 'Okay, Ron.' He was delighted he was going to do the darting.

'Those are exceedingly treacherous nyamazans and they can kill you very dead and if I hear you've taken any risks so help me I'll kick your arse all the way back to Salisbury,' Thompson said.

'Yes, Ron,' Richard said. 'Okay, Ron.'

We were sitting round Thompson's fire and he had his blue swollen ankle up on a foot-rest. 'Coetsee is Coetsee. You're Richard Peek, twenty years old with the popular number of holes in your body and you want to stay that way.'

'Definitely, Ron.'

'If I hear you've taken any risks you know what I'll do?'

'You'll kick my arse all the way back to Salisbury,' said Richard.

'And I'll kick your arse right into Head Office into Filing Section,' Thompson said, 'and that's where you'll stay.'

A fate worse than death. 'Okay, Ron.'

Richard was Thompson's blue-eyed boy. 'Remember what the soothsayer told Coetsee. It's all rubbish but just you remember it. And remember what I'll do.'

Richard was as keen as mustard and if Thompson had taken it into his head to kick his arse all the way back to Salisbury right here and now just to impress it upon him, it would have been all right with young Richard, just so long as he was allowed to get his hands on the dart-gun tomorrow.

CHAPTER SIXTEEN

IT was a beautiful Rhodesian bush morning, bright and crisp and golden and we were sweating already in the chill dry riverbed that led up into the hills from Old Norman's camp. Young Richard had very long legs and he was as fit as a thoroughly healthy young game ranger can be and he was striding through the heavy river-sand that came over the tops of your boots each step, and Old Norman's game scout who was leading us to the spoor was having a hard job keeping ahead of him. 'He's just two miles up the river-bed,' Old Norman had said, 'tied up by the tail to a tree for you.'

'Yes, Mr. Payn,' Richard had said. 'Thank you, Mr. Payn.'

'I've just been speaking to Mr. Thompson on the roger-roger,' Old Norman had said, 'and he says to remind you what he'll do if you take any risks.'

'Yes, Mr. Payn,' Richard had said. 'Thank you, Mr. Payn,' and he waved to us like a cavalry officer to follow him and he went striding up the river-bed almost as fast, and dearly I wished that Thompson hadn't sprained his ankle. Thompson was more my vintage. After two miles of this river-sand and dearly wishing that Thompson hadn't sprained his bloody ankle, the game scout signalled a halt. He panted that a chip-imbiri was near this place. We were all panting and sweating, the game scouts, Graham Hall and Nevin and all, that heart-thudding, trembling muscular exhausting that river-sand gives you, all except young Richard. There was a whispered consultation between Richard and the game scout in which I took no interest. I was interested in nothing except lying flat out on my back on the river-sand. Then they started carefully on up the river-bed and we heaved ourselves up to follow.

We crept one hundred yards panting up the winding river-bed, and then we saw him. He was out in the open only one hundred yards up the long low hill that ran down to the river. This was very lucky: this was very lucky indeed, the wind was right, the cover was right the river-sand had muffled our foot-steps, everything. We crouched down in the river-bed. Richard was getting his first rhino handed to him on a plate. And I was very grateful indeed that we were not going to be tracking all day with Richard with those bloody legs. He was loading the dart-gun excitedly, whispering orders. We were so close that we were all to stay in the cover of the bank of the river, except Hall with the .458 to give him cover. And young Richard went in after his first rhino.

He crept quickly crouched through the tall grass downwind for a bit, very excited, then he paused to test the wind, then he circled in towards the beast. He did not have far to go to get within decent range. We could see both him and the beast clearly, from our cover on the river-bank. The beast had not moved. Behind it was thick tall grass, and if it moved into that Richard would be in trouble. If he did not go in after it he would lose it, and if he did Thompson would kick his arse all the way back to Salisbury. So far he was dead lucky, the beast was just standing there but he had no time to waste, at any moment the beast might move into the tall grass. Richard got within forty yards, and the beast was just standing there still, oblivious, sideways on, a perfect target and young Richard raised the dart-gun and you could almost see him shaking with excitement, and he squeezed the trigger, and the gun went click.

Click, *the bloody gun went click, the unmentionable cartridge was another bloody dud the second bloody time.* Richard was shaking as he opened the breach and yanked out the adaptor and rammed in another cartridge. The rhino heard the click and spun round, ears forward, horn up, glaring, forty paces from Richard. Then he turned again and glared in the opposite direction, but now he was a bad target. He lumbered towards the thick tall grass and I thought, *There he bloody goes*, then he stopped. He turned round once more, his ears going in all directions, then he relaxed and put his ears back. And he was a perfect target again and I was gabbling prayers wildly and Richard squeezed off again. And *it bloody well went bloody click again.*

It bloody well went bloody click again and the beast spun around ears up all horn and snort and looking for something to kill and Richard was cursing, fumbling to open the breach and ram another cartridge in and the beast lumbered three paces towards him glaring and snorting and looked around murderously, *glared straight at the grass Richard was hiding in and Richard was fumbling with the new cartridge shaking and curs-*

ing – and the rhino turned round. He turned and went lumbering straight at the tall thick grass again, straight towards it and I thought, *Now there he really goes* and cursed the cartridge manufacturers, and then he stopped again. He stopped and looked round once more. Then he just stood. God, this was lucky. Then he *relaxed again*. And then he *lay down*. He lay *down?* God, *this was luck*, somebody up there really liked young Richard, the beast *lay down* and Richard was shaking and he raised the gun, and he fired. And there was the crack of the cartridge and the big dart flew true. It smacked with a flash into the great beast's side and he scrambled up furiously snorting, and there was a great crashing in the grass and *suddenly there were bloody rhinos all over the place*.

Bloody rhinos everywhere, great crashing of grass and thundering of the earth and snorting and out of the grass they came crashing and thundering spread over a hundred yards, four adult prehistoric rhinos plus Richard's, charging snorting thundering straight down at us in the river-bed, and we scrambled. We scrambled in all directions, black and white scrambling everywhere running jumping running for our lives leaping for the trees, shouting, getting the hell out of it the most primitive feeling in the world, running tripping scrambling for the trees you didn't care if you gouged both eyes out tore both ears off or who you trampled underfoot just so long as you got up that bloody tree before those thundering horns got your arse. I ran flat out for the nearest tree and it was built as unhelpfully as a telephone pole, I looked back once wildly and all I saw was terrible rhinos and one two-thousand-pounder in particular aggrieved as all get-out head down thundering straight at my arse, and that tree built like a telephone pole was no trouble at all. No trouble at *all*, I ran up that telephone tree like a rabbit, head first into the straggling black backside – '*Get up the bloody tree!*' I screamed and the struggling black backside stood on my head scrambling up but it would have taken strong machinery to get me out of that tree and I was scrambling up after the scrambling black backside. And the beast thundered past underneath me, hooking and snorting, and the earth shook. They went thundering on up the river-bank all together huffing and puffing, great grey legs pounding and their tails curled up over their backs, very impressive and invincible. And they were gone.

I looked around, and all the trees were festooned with grinning bodies. I looked for Richard and he was coming down out of a tree. I slid down my tree, and my palms and fingertips were scored open, and I was shaking with nerves and laughter. We were all laughing. It must have been a record: rhinos don't go in herds like that.

Richard came up shaking, grinning all over his face with the whole thing – '*I thought that soothsayer was going to be right.*'

I don't go much on witch-doctors and soothsayers but I remember I thought: touch wood.

CHAPTER SEVENTEEN

IT was only two o'clock when the Mercedes got us back to the stockade at Nyamasota. Thompson was very pleased with Richard. Richard was very pleased with himself. We were all very pleased. Thompson stood on the top of the stockade on his good leg supervising Richard down there in the pen. I was beside Thompson with my camera, I was going to take photographs of Richard fixing up his first rhinoceros. It was a fine bull. He looked very good lying there, sweating, groaning, fast asleep, flat out on his side. He was five feet six inches at the shoulder, and his horn was twenty-nine inches long. That gave him a reach of eight or nine feet high.

Richard was doing a good job down there. He had done a good job all day. The beast had been unconscious for nearly five hours, it was due to come round naturally from the drug and Richard did not have much time. The animal had already tried once to get up, a great, asthmatic, wild-eyed thrashing against the ropes and crashing his head, but everybody had piled on him and brought him down and he had passed out again. Richard had already earmarked him, he lay now collapsed next to the mopani fence, bloody-eared, great legs lashed with rope and five labourers were on top of him, one standing on his bull neck holding on to the poles, two sitting on his spine and one on his shoulder and one on his haunches, while Richard prepared to give him the antidote of nalorphine. He took the phial out of the *muti*-box held it up against the sunlight and filled the syringe. Then he closed the *muti*-box and carried it to the edge of the pen and handed the box up to a game scout. Then he stabbed the needle into the thick hide with a thump. The beast twitched his ears once at the prick then groaned back to sleep. Richard screwed the syringe on to the needle. Then he said in Chilapalapa:

'Loosen the knots. Do not untie them completely, only loosen them so that you can undo them easily after the injection.'

One labourer loosened the knots. Richard watched him, crouched over the syringe at the beast's rump. It took half a minute. We all watched. Graham Hall was standing directly above Richard, on a cross-member, just out of reach of the horn of the beast in the next pen, below his feet.

The native loosened the knots, Richard pressed the syringe plunger and the antidote went in. The labourers were still standing and sitting on the beast. Richard opened his mouth to tell the African to untie the knots and Thompson shouted:

'Have you given him his penicillin?'

'No'! young Richard said, shocked at himself.

'Well, you better make it snappy.' It was the only mistake young Richard had made all day.

'*Fasten the knots!*' Richard shouted at the African and he ran to the fence for the *muti*-box.

The game scout handed the box down to him. Richard grabbed another syringe and the penicillin bottle, held both up to the skyline and filled the syringe. We watched him. He snapped the box closed and handed it back up to the game scout. Then he ran back to the animal. It was still fast asleep.

He thumped the needle into the beast's rump. Everybody still had their weight on the animal, and it did not even twitch. It was fast asleep. Richard screwed the syringe on to the needle, and he depressed the plunger, he got it half-way down and the animal came round with a thrash.

It came round without a flicker of warning and thrashed its great neck and head and horn and the knots had not been tightened properly and the great legs thrashed free and Thompson screamed, '*Watch out!*' The big bull thrashed wild-eyed and his vicious horn crashed and the man on his neck leapt up the fence like a monkey and the man on his back and shoulder scattered across the pen kicking dust and Richard yanked the half-empty syringe out of the beast, in a flash the great beast swung up on to his feet, vicious, red-eyed, looking for somebody to kill *and there were plenty to kill*, Africans scattering all over the pen and Richard reeling back clutching the syringe and the vicious man-high red-eyed one-ton beast whirling round and Thompson screamed, '*Get out!*' and Africans scrambled all over the place, and Richard leapt for the fence. He leapt shocked, long-legged, still clutching the syringe, one arm outstretched, one long leg swinging up to the cross-member and he was clinging, clawing like that half-way up the fence, clutching the syringe when the beast hit him.

The beast swung its massive head and horn up his back, thirty inches of sharp horn and two thousand pounds behind it flashing up at his kidneys, Richard arched his back clawing up the fence and the killer horn flashed past his shirt miraculously, in a flash the beast swiped its horn again and it smashed

116

through Richard's swinging leg. Right through the leg, sharp thirty-inch horn swiped on massive bull neck straight through the back of Richard's calf and out at the shinbone, Richard clung wildly half-way up the fence, aghast, still clutching the syringe and the beast could have hooked him, could have flicked its head back and plucked Richard off the fence and killed him in one go, could have flung him twenty feet over the stockade very dead with his guts hanging out, could have swung Richard off the fence in a trice. Thompson screamed, '*Grab him!*' and Graham Hall was lunging along the top of the stockade and grabbed down at Richard and heaved and the beast yanked out its horn and hit him again. It lashed up at Richard's leg as Hall yanked Richard up by the shirt and the rhino cow on Hall's side of the stockade charged and crashed the poles and everybody was shouting, And Richard's bull hit his hanging foot. Smashed him on his boot a glancing blow with many times the force of a sharp sledge-hammer and smashed the tissue and blood-vessels and muscles and it swung its massive head to hit him again properly and Hall heaved Richard up out of reach on to the cross-member, shocked clinging, bloody, with the big hole through his leg and still clutching the damn syringe and everybody was shouting and the beast spun round looking for somebody else to kill, and it spun on two natives standing there petrified.

The beast spun and Thompson screamed, '*Get out of the pen!*' and one of the natives just stood transfixed, terrified, staring at the beast turning on him four feet away. '*Get out of the pen!*' Thompson screamed and the second native also stood transfixed, terrified witless, and for a split second the beast paused gathering to charge at the first native's guts just four feet in front of him and there was going to be blood and guts smashed all over the pen – '*Get out of the pen!*' Thompson screamed and the second African regained his wits and scrambled and the beast swung from the first man's guts and charged the second man. The native fled across the pen with the beast pounding after him head down to kill and the first native regained his terrified wits and he scrambled also, *he ran the same way as the beast was charging, alongside the killer beast in his witless terror* and then he fell, crashed headlong, terrified witless, in the dust beside the thundering hooves and scrambled up, dust flying, frantic and the second man threw himself at the fence and somebody grabbed him and the beast crashed its horn into the fence six inches from his clambering legs, then it spun around to look for the first man. And he was scrambling up the far corner, it charged thundering across the pen at him, but it was too late. The whole thing had taken about eight seconds.

Richard was hopping along the cross-member on his good leg, clutching the top of the stockade, still holding the syringe, and Hall was scrambling alongside him still hanging on to his shirt and in all four pens the rhinos were snorting and charging and crashing the poles in the bloody pandemonium and everybody was shouting. I jumped down from the top of the stockade and Thompson jumped also. I ran round the stockade to where Richard and Hall were clambering and Thompson was hopping after me flat out on one leg shouting for the *muti*-box. As I got round the stockade Richard was swinging his gored leg over the top of the stockade to jump and his face was dead white, screwed up in shocked pain and he shouted to Thompson hopping behind me, '*This ruins my darting*,' and he jumped. He landed on his good leg and I got my shoulder under his armpit and he hopped beside me hanging on.

'*This ruins my darting—*'

'Lie down!'

He let go and collapsed on to his back, face white, screwed up, wild with pain and there was the gaping hole right through his leg, a great four-inch crescent gaping flesh and fat and blood and muscle and bone and hair, he struggled to sit up to look at it then collapsed back, aghast – '*Just when I've started darting—*'

'*Muti!*' Thompson bellowed.

'*Oh God this ruins the darting!*' Ben came running with the *muti*-box. '*Are you going to kick my arse all the way back to Salisbury?*' His face was screwed up, he was biting his knuckle, wild-eyed.

'I'm going to give you morphine.'

'*Oh God what about the darting?*'

Thompson snapped the tip off the nozzled phial of morphine and I gripped Richard's leg and Thompson slapped the needle into his thigh and squirted the morphine into him. Richard jerked and clutched his thigh.

'Get him to the tents.'

I heaved him up on one elbow and Hall grabbed the other and we got his arms round our necks. The blood was welling up out of the fatty wound now and running over his boot. He started hopping flat out for the tents hanging on to us, face screwed up, panting, gasping.

Thompson was hopping ahead of us flat out for the tents. When we got there he was hopping round filling a basin with Dettol, throwing a big wad of lint into it. We collapsed Richard into a camp-chair and put another under his leg, he was gasping. There was blood everywhere now, everybody was gathered round, aghast. Thompson slapped the cold Dettol-soaked lint on to the big wound and Richard screamed and clutched his knee, face screwed up.

'Who's got the fastest vehicle?'

'I have,' I said.

'*I thought you were going to kick my arse all the way back to Salisbury,*' Richard gasped, clutching his leg.

'Yes please,' Thompson said to me.

I ran through the long grass up to my tents. I slung all my stuff out of the station wagon. 'Bring me some fruit. Pillows. Blankets. Cigarettes. Four bottles of beer.' I shouted to Brightspark Tafurandika. I started the engine and went crashing, bouncing, through the tall grass down to Thompson's tents.

When I got there he was finishing bandaging the lint over the wound.

'How's the morphine?'

'It hasn't started yet.'

Brightspark Tafurandika came running through the grass carrying the things I had told him.

'Who needs a beer?' I said. I sure needed one. Richard unscrewed his eyes and grabbed the bottle out of my hands, gasping. '*You shouldn't drink after that shock!*' I said, and he rammed the bottle neck into his mouth and crunched the cap off with his teeth in one agonized go and spat out the cap and thrust the bottle back in my hands with his face screwed up again and his hands clutched back at his knee. He hadn't wanted a drink, he only wanted to bite on something. '*Oh Gard!*' he shouted at the pain.

'Let's get going.'

We carried Richard to my station wagon. He tried to hop but the blood rushing down to the wound when he stood up made him shout. The morphine had not worked yet. We put him across the back seat with his leg up and supported him with pillows. Thompson got into the front seat beside me. I revved the engine and let out the clutch. We churned ten yards through the grass and Thompson shouted at me to stop. He stuck his head out the window.

'*Who knows the path to Mount Darwin?*'

'Nkosi.' The old *manzi*-man put up his hand.

'Get in, Gunga Din.'

The old *manzi*-man clambered into the back of the station wagon. I set off bouncing down the tracks out of Nyamasota.

'*God, I'm sorry,*' Richard gasped.

'Forget it, boy,' Thompson said.

'*It was my fault – I should have remembered the penicillin—*'

'I was supervising you.'

'*You trusted me. You trusted me, God I'm sorry—*'

'It was the African's fault,' I said, 'he didn't tighten the knots again properly.' I was driving hard as I could, bouncing on the tracks.

'*I should have checked the ropes myself,*' Richard gasped. I could see him in the rear-view mirror, he was clutching his leg wincing with each bounce, face screwed up.

'You're entitled to assume other people have done their job.'

'Which one was it?' Thompson said.

'I can't remember.' I was driving as hard as I could, bouncing, swinging the wheel, the dust flying behind us.

'*I'd like to kick his arse all the way back to Salisbury. Just when I was starting darting.*'

'You see?' Thompson said. 'You see what bloody treacherous animals they are?'

'And fast.' I was driving hard, we were all unwinding from the tension.

'*You've no idea how big they are until one's having a go at you down there.*'

'You see what I mean?' Thompson said. 'You see why I don't hunt like Coetsee?'

'That rhino moved fast,' I said, 'greased lightning.'

'Now you see what I mean, I've had too many close shaves with them not to treat them with the greatest bloody respect.'

'*The soothsayer was right,*' Richard groaned, '*that soothsayer was bloody well right—*'

'Rubbish,' Thompson said.

'*Well I've had mine,*' Richard groaned. '*That's my lot.*'

'Is that as far as you're prepared to go to please a writer?' I said.

CHAPTER EIGHTEEN

It was dark by the time we saw the few lights of Mount Darwin far away over the bush. It had taken three hours, skidding, bouncing, jolting, driving flat out. The morphine had worked, for a while the pain had almost gone and young Richard was euphoric, talking loudly even laughing sometimes; for a time it had all seemed to him like some kind of bad joke under the morphine and Thompson and I drank the four beers and jollied him along. Then the morphine had worn off and he had started gasping and groaning again, clutching his knee tight and the jolting of the car agonized him. I could see him screwing up his face in the rear-view mirror and sometimes he shouted cursing at the pain and he had his brush hat stuffed in his mouth biting it, and we just drove hard through the bush, hardly talking. The bandage was soaked red with blood now and his foot where the beast had hit him was swollen up big and blue-black. We were bloody glad to see the lights of Mount Darwin and the lights of the small African hospital on the outskirts. I roared down the dirt road and swung into the hospital gate churning on the gravel and already an African nurse was coming down the steps towards us. Graham Hall had radioed Head Office and Head Office had telephoned Mount Darwin. I swung the car up to the hospital steps, nearly running over the nurse. Thompson leapt out of the car and went hopping on his good leg up the hospital steps to find the doctor. The nurse and I got Richard out of the back seat and he cried out when the blood flowed back down his leg.

It was a small, old hospital building, corrugated iron roof and wide cement verandahs with African patients sitting

around taking the air. We hobbled Richard, gasping, up the steps and along the verandah and the African patients stared at us. The European medical orderly appeared in his white surgery tunic with Thompson hopping beside him. There was no doctor in Mount Darwin. We got Richard through the french doors into the small surgery that opened on to the verandah. We got Richard up on the table and he cried out, biting into his hat.

'A small matter of a rhino?' the medic said. He was a tough-looking Kiwi and he had a cigarette in his mouth.

'I gave him morphine,' Thompson said. We were very dirty, covered in dust. Richard was lying there, wild-eyed, stuffing his hat in his mouth.

'How you guys getting on out there?' The medic was unwrapping the blood-soaked bandage. Richard cried out with each touch jerking on the table.

'Fine.' The medic peeled off the last strip of bandage and there was the big bloody wrapping of lint and Richard jerked and gargled through his hat.

'Chuck this out for me, sport.' He handed me his cigarette. I threw it out the french doors into the night and three African patients scrambled for it. Richard was gasping, ashen under the dust, sweating, his face looked waxen, and Thompson was leaning across his stomach to hold him down. 'Let's give it a glare.' He lifted the bloody lint off and Richard screamed and Thompson held him tight, and there it was, and I felt my guts go pale. It was bigger than I remembered, gaping and crescent-shaped where the horn had come out and you could see the bone and muscles and globules of fat hanging and the hairy skin around it was blue-black-grey and dead-looking and the hole at the back of the leg must be bigger and my guts went dead pale. I gripped Richard's elbow, he was writhing, biting his hat. 'So you guys catchin' lots of rhino out there?' the medic said. 'Open my case,' he said to the African nurse. She was wearing a black wig under her white cap.

'*You're going to give me an anaesthetic first?*' Richard shouted.

'I haven't gone near you yet.'

'You like it in this country, doc?' Thompson said leaning hard across Richard's guts.

'Sure.' The nurse was having trouble, I took the black bag from her and opened it. 'How many rhino have you caught?'

'Fourteen.' I wanted to shout: *Shut up about rhinos and give this poor bastard an anaesthetic!* The medic got out a bottle and syringe and held it up to the light, he was not wasting time in fact.

'He's giving you some M99,' I said. He was sweating, his knuckle stuffed in his mouth.

'Got tired of your hat?' the medic said, coming with the syringe. 'Give us your arm, sport, stick your other knuckle in your mouth.'

I took his arm and gave him his hat to bite, he stuffed it in his mouth and flung his head the other way. 'Hold his arm tight.' I held it and he stuck the needle straight into a vein.

'How do you find the vein so easily?' Thompson said. 'I have to poke around on rhinos.'

'I'm not much cop on rhinos myself,' the medic said modestly. 'Never had them in New Zealand.'

'Good fishing in New Zealand?' Thompson said.

'Great fishing.' He was washing his hands, Richard was writhing biting his hat, I held his hand tight.

'What did you give him?'

'Pethedine. Great fishing.'

'Trout?'

'Beaut trout. Gloves,' he said to the African nurse with the wig.

'Oh God,' Richard writhed.

'Marvellous trout,' pulling on the rubber gloves, they stretched like brown skin over his hands. 'He missed the bone.'

124

'It was so bloody nearly his kidneys, you should have seen it.'

'This'll be a bit cold.' He began to swab the leg with yellow disinfectant and Richard screamed and Thompson and I held him tight. 'Do you ski?'

'No,' Thompson said.

'Good skiing, in New Zealand.' He swabbed the whole leg yellow from the knee down to between his toes with Richard jerking, then he wiped over the ragged edges of the wound and he screamed again. 'The pethedine will fix you up. How do you feel?'

'Bloody terrible,' Richard gritted, ashen-white, crunching my hand.

'Hold tight,' the medic nodded, and he swabbed into the wound and Richard screamed and bucked on the table and I leant my arm across the poor bastard's heaving chest and Thompson grabbed his knee. 'No, *no!*' the medic said to Thompson, '*don't touch his leg with your grubby paws, now I'll have to re-swab the whole leg.*'

'Sorry,' Thompson said.

'Can't take you anywhere,' the medic said and began to swab the leg again. 'Okay,' he said to Richard, 'I won't stick it in the wound again,' and I thought, *Thank God*.

'Now for a spot of sewing.'

'*Oh God,*' Richard writhed, '*give me an injection.*'

'Sure-sure,' the medic said.

'*But not into the wound, please not into the wound—*'

'Okay, sport, okay.' He picked up a long-needled syringe and glanced to make sure Thompson was blocking Richard's view. 'Yes, New Zealand is beautiful,' and he slid the needle into the open wound and Richard writhed *Aarrh – aarrh* and crunched my hand and flung his head and I felt myself go pale, 'Beautiful,' the medic withdrew the needle, 'and boring,' and slid it in again a quarter of an inch along and pumped more anaesthetic in and Richard cried out and Thompson and I held him.

125

'Why boring?' Thompson said.

The medic put the needle in at another place. 'Nothing more important to argue about than the price of butter—'

'*Aaarh!*' Richard screamed.

'And lamb chops,' the medic said. 'And cheese,' he continued, injecting at quarter inch intervals, 'and so forth,' and Richard bucked and we held him down and I could feel myself white and a ringing in my ears. 'Whereas here,' he injected, 'there's a bit of history in the making,' he chose another spot, 'and all that jazz—' Richard was gasping out, face screwed up, sweating, writhing, biting his hat. 'If you like that sort of thing. Turn on your side, sport.'

'*Oh Garrd!*' Richard said.

We held him on his side and the medic started injecting into the hole in the back of the leg and Richard shouted, '*Garrrd!*'

'You look a bit white,' the medic said to me.

'I feel a bit white.'

'The other day,' he injected, 'a cop brought an African in to be stitched up and,' he selected, 'the cop passed out cold.'

He told us about the cop while he finished injecting into the hind wound and we held Richard tight. The pethedine began to work well and he stopped writhing and jerking so much, just groaning and sweating and biting his hat and his hair stuck matted to his forehead and we did not have to hold him so tight but he still crunched my hand. By the time the stitching started Richard was quieter. The medic took the big hooked needle and thread and he held up a flap of flesh with forceps and forced it through and Richard jerked and I felt sicker.

'Did you feel that?'

'*A bit,*' Richard gasped.

'No,' the medic said, 'the outside is asleep, you're feeling the pain that's down deep in the wound. Think about your girl friend.'

'You better think about your girl friend too,' he said to me.

'Okay,' I said.

He carried on stitching. He sewed twenty-nine stitches and I thought it would never stop, but Richard stopped feeling it and after that the right colour came back to my face a bit and the wound looked a hell of a lot better all stitched up.

That night I drove Richard on to Salisbury.

It was dark when Thompson and I got back into Nyamasota the next night. When I got to my tents Brightspark Tafurandika was not anywhere around. I shouted for him, furious. I was very tired and hungry. Then I got myself a beer out of the bag angrily and sat down in my camp-chair by my fire. When I was half-way through the beer Brightspark Tafurandika appeared. He had an alarmed chicken tucked under his armpit.

'*Where have you been?*'

'I have been buying us a chicken, Nkosi,' he said injuredly.

'You've been to a bloody beerdrink!'

Brightspark Tafurandika looked hurt. 'I don't drink beer, myself. I bought us this nice chicken.' He tripped over a guy-rope and fell on all fours and the chicken took to its legs. It went flapping, squawking, horrified across the camp, legged it round the fire and disappeared into the night grass thankfully. Brightspark Tafurandika scrambled up and legged after it shouting strong invective. I had no idea the old basket could move so fast. He disappeared crashing into the grass yelling at the chicken to come back. The crashing went on for a minute, then it stopped. He restored to honeyed cooing and clucking noises to entice it back. The cooing and clucking went on for a bit, then Brightspark Tafurandika came stomping back. 'Now make my bath and skoff,' I said in Chilapalapa.

He looked back over the grass into the night after the chicken, disgusted.

'How is the young European?' he said, disgusted with the chicken.

'He is all right.'

'Did the doctor put stitches in him?'

'Many,' I said.

'Hey-*hey* . . .' Brightspark shook his head, 'the witch-doctor was right that he would be injured.'

'That is nonsense,' I said. 'Witch-doctors are nonsense.'

Brightspark Tafurandika looked at me, shocked.

'Witch-doctors are not nonsense! As true as God is in the sky.'

'God?' I looked up at the sky elaborately. 'Where is God; I don't see Him.'

'God is on the moon,' Brightspark Tafurandika said.

'The *moon*?' I said. 'But the Americans went to the moon and they did not see one god.'

Brightspark Tafurandika stared at me in the firelight.

'Do you,' he said slowly, 'believe that nonsense?'

'What nonsense?' I said.

'That the Americans went to the moon,' Brightspark Tafurandika said.

'Of course,' I said.

Brightspark Tafurandkia stared at me incredulously for a moment.

'Ah!' he said regretfully.

'Don't you believe it?' I said.

'*Believe* it?' Brightspark Tafurandika said. 'Of course I don't believe it! Only women and young men would believe that.'

'But there are photographs,' I said, 'ma-fotos.'

'Ma-*fotos*,' Brightspark Tafurandika said, very disappointed in me and the chicken. 'That is just a story to make the Russians unhappy.'

I said, 'Have the Russians reached the moon?'

Brightspark looked at me, disgusted.

'No man can reach the moon, Nkosi. Because it is impossible.'

'Oh,' I said. 'But you believe in witch-doctors?'

Brightspark Tafurandika exasperated, 'What did the witch-doctor say about the first European who was killed? What did he say about the young European of yesterday?'

He looked at me. He shook his black finger at me in the firelight.

'You better be careful, Nkosi. Your hair is also a little yellow.'

'Not very,' I said.

'Quite a lot yellow in the sun. And the next man to be caught by a chipimbiri has yellow hair.'

'Are you worried about getting your wages?' I said.

I do not go much on soothsayers and witch-doctors, but Fosbury was dead and young Richard had got his, and I was very glad indeed I am not very blond, not like Thompson and Coetsee and Nevin.

Part Four

CHAPTER NINETEEN

AT the end of August it was really the end of the long dry
winter and it was getting very much hotter in the Ruya on the
Mozambique border, the hard, hot earth hotter and harder and
the dry bush dryer and the shade was only the skeletons of the
bush, and the dust was dustier and in the dry river-beds the sun
beat up off the sand at you. In one month, maybe six weeks, the
big rains would come, when the earth was almost dead, and
then Operation Rhino would have to stop. In late August the
Operation was very nearly finished in the Ruya. There were
very few rhino left, we had nearly got them all out, and now, in
the last week of that August, the spoor was getting very hard to
find; the rhino were getting very nervous because they knew
they were being hunted, the game scouts went a long way out
into the hard hot hills from Old Norman's camp before they
found any spoor, and when we got on to it the beast had gone a
very long way indeed and it was late in the afternoon when we
made contact and darted him and long after midnight when we
got him back to Nyamasota.

At the beginning of that last week we reckoned there were
only three chipimbiri left in the Ruya, according to the spoor, a
cow with a half-grown calf and the old bull who lived by himself very close to the Mozambique border, the one the natives
said was white in colour. We had seen his spoor, but we had not
seen him. It was a big spoor. We were very excited to think that

maybe he really was albino, like the natives said, but we did not believe it. Nobody has ever reported an albino rhinocerous. It was probably only mud. We got on to the spoor of the calf and cow, and they were heading in the direction of the border and then we saw that there was spoor of two adults and the calf, running together. We followed that spoor all day and we did not see them and night came.

The next day we went back at first light to the place where we had left off and we picked up the spoor again. Late in the afternoon we saw them, the cow and a calf and a bull, and the bull did look white. We stared at them, a hundred and twenty yards off, we could only just make them out over the grass, but the bull did look rather white. It could be mud but it must be most unusual mud. Maybe we really were going to capture the first albino rhinoceros in the world.

We crouched there, watching and sweating. That they were together meant either that they were mating or that they were frightened, knew they were being hunted right out. The wind was with us. They were alert and nervous, but they could not see us. We could have tried to dart both cow and bull, for we had two guns, but there was not enough light left to track both animals if they ran in different directions. Whereas if we darted the cow and calf, they would run together. It was a great pity that we could not get the bull also today, it would be very hard finding him again. Thompson and Hall set off stalking down on them and we stayed back, watching. The bull was very alert all the time, with the responsibility of the cow and the calf, but there was good cover and the wind was with us. Thompson and Hall got down to within sixty yards of the cow and the calf, but they still could not tell yet if the bull was really albino. It was a great pity that they could not dart both cow and bull. They loosed off at the cow and calf simultaneously on a signal and the darts flew home, and they all ran.

They ran thundering off, all three together, and we started tracking immediately. The three spoors stayed together for maybe one mile, then the calf began to go down, and the cow fell back to stay with it. The bull stayed back for them, then the cow began to go down also, the bull's spoor stayed with them some time, then he ran on.

We found the calf first and then, half a mile on, the cow. The big white bull, the last rhino in the Ruya, had gone.

CHAPTER TWENTY

THE next day we went out after him long before light. The stars were still bright in black sky. It was just beginning to dawn when we got to Old Norman's camp on the Ruya, we were very cold from riding on the back of the Mercedes. Old Norman had already sent two game scouts out, on the chance that the animal might have moved back towards our part of the Ruya in the night, but we were going to trek back to the place where the cow had fallen yesterday, to pick up his spoor from there. It was very important that we get him before he went across the border into Mozambique, where the Ruya became the Luia, and anything goes. If we did not get him, because he had become too wild, Operation Rhino would have come back for him next year after the rains. All for one animal. If the poachers did not get him. While we were drinking tea round the early morning fire Old Norman called Thompson aside and they had a whispered conversation, then they went into Old Norman's tent. When Thompson came out he looked very pleased about something, and I guessed it was about Norman's poaching investigations. Nobody ever knew what Old Norman was doing, or when he was going to do it, or how he did it, until he was about to do it.

It took us three hours hard walking to get back to the place the cow had fallen. We picked up his spoor and we followed the spoor all that day, we lost it then picked it up many times, we followed him into the very late afternoon, but we did not see him. We did not even see any fresh sign, no wet dung or urine, and he had not lain down in the middle of the day, he passed several dust-bowls but he kept moving. It was very hot. He knew he was being hunted. He knew, all right. He had been running with the cow and calf and he knew. The only good thing about that day was that he did not head towards the Mozambique border. He made wide swoops over the hills and valleys, but when we knocked off in the late afternoon, because soon it would be too dark to track, he was heading back into the Rhodesian hills. It was dark when we got back to Old Norman's camp and he was working in his tent over a big pile of papers by lamplight and he and Thompson talked aside again, then we got on to the Mercedes, very tired and pretty tired of the Ruya, and went back to Nyamasota.

The next day we went out again, to the place where we had left the spoor, we found it but after three hours tracking we lost it. We looked for it until late into the afternoon but we did not find it again that day. It was 29th August, in two days Coetsee must come back to take over the Operation, transferring camp back to Mususumoya; it needed two days to move camp that distance over that country, and after finishing there again Coetsee would have to move camp again to Gokwe and that would take another two or three days, and there were not many days left before the rains came. We should have given up the white bull that second bad day, but Thompson very much wanted that last bull, to clean up the whole Ruya. And to see if he was really white.

'One more day,' Thompson told Old Norman. 'Tomorrow.'

It was still dark when we got to Old Norman's camp on the Ruya the next day. Only his cookboy was there.

CHAPTER TWENTY-ONE

ALL the poachers knew that today was the last day the white men would hunt, that tomorrow they would leave the Ruya. The poachers had been very careful where they set their snares and where they hid their horns and hides and how they disposed of the meat, and some had lain very low in their kraals and not poached at all, and none had dared use their rifles and old muzzle-loaders whilst the white men were in the Ruya in such numbers, but all the same the poachers thought the white men and their game scouts were very stupid for not finding anything, particularly for not finding even one of the three camp sites of the poachers who came from a long way to poach there every winter when most rivers were dry and all the animals moved to the Ruya to drink. It was still long before first light of that last day when Old Norman hit them.

Old Norman had divided his game scouts into parties and they set out in Land-Rovers and on foot and on bicycles in different directions when it was still night, and each party knew precisely where they were going and who they were after and what evidence they already had against each and what else to look for, and the poachers never knew what hit them. Old Norman and his men caught them while they lay in their blankets and squatted round their early-morning fires, one after the other they took over the three camp sites hidden in the far hills and simultaneously over a twenty mile radius other parties were going for the poachers from the Ruya who were lying low in their kraals; one after another from camp to camp and kraal to kraal Old Norman and his men swooped in rapid succession that day in Land-Rover and on cycle and on foot faster than the word could spread on the bush telegraph. Old Norman and his men set out to arrest thirty-six men that day, and only one man got away.

It was hot already at nine o'clock that last day when we picked up the spoor of the white bull. Maybe it was going to be a lucky day. It was good spoor too, early morning's, not yesterday's. We were only a few hours behind him, and there was very little wind. Maybe it was going to be a lucky last day.

At noon we made contact with him. He had kept moving all morning, but he had eluded us for two days and in the heat of noon he had thought he was safe to lie up for a while. We came over the top of a rise and there we saw him a hundred and twenty yards down, standing in some hot sparse shade, hindquarters into the wind. *Down*, Thompson signalled, *Down, down, down!* and we all went right down flat, sweating and excited. This really was a lucky day. We lay there bloody glad it was the last day in the Ruya, and Thompson tested the wind with the ash-bag, and it was right, then he started down the slope. The bull looked very big and white and I thought excitedly that maybe we were wrong about it being mud, maybe he really was an albino, the first albino Black Rhino in the world. We were very excited watching Thompson creep down the slope through the bush; ninety yards, eighty yards, seventy, and still the old bull stood there tail into the wind ears going in all directions, sixty yards, and Thompson was nearly in safe range. Fifty-five yards, and then fifty, and Thompson raised the gun to fire, and the beast spun around and faced him. He jerked around at Thompson ears cocked, and took one snorting look, and then turned and fled. He ran off huffing and puffing as hard as he could with his tail curled up over his huge off-white haunches, crashing through the grass, and was gone.

'*After him!*' Thompson mouthed.

The atmosphere was pretty blue. We ran after him through the grass to the place where he had gone on out of sight and then picked up the spoor; we followed him as fast as we could but we could only track at walking pace, and he was running. It was very hot, and the atmosphere was pretty blue all right.

We tracked him eighteen miles that afternoon. He kept moving almost all the time. The only good thing was that he was not running for the Portuguese border. We tracked him as hard as we could reliably go, sweating, tired, tired of the Ruya, the heat, the tracking, this bull. The only thing that consoled us was that maybe he really was an albino, maybe. Thompson did not think so and he had been closest of all of us. The natives swore he was albino. We made contact with him twice again that afternoon, and he ran. He took one look and ran, he did not stick around to huff and puff and roll his bloodshot eyes, he just put back his big ears and curled up his tail and ran. The poor old bastard knew man was after him and he knew all the other rhino were gone, and he was very frightened. The first time we made contact in the afternoon was over another rise and again we all fell flat – *down down down* – and Thompson stalked him, but he did not get closer than eighty yards before the beast heard him, or smelt him, and ran. The second time was over another rise, he must have stopped to feed at the bottom of the valley and that is why we had gained on him, but he was over a mile away, just heading at a big hard trot up the far slope the other side of the valley all by himself through the hot yellow afternoon sun. It was impossible for him to have seen us or heard us or smelt us, he was just frightened and keeping moving, heading nowhere, just running. But this second time the direction he was running was the Portuguese border.

We were very tired. We took bearings on some rocks on the top of the far slope where he had disappeared; we ran down our side of the valley as fast as we could, loping, jumping over rocks, round trees, through the grass, panting and sweating, down into the valley, scrambling across the ravine where he had been feeding, up the other side, running for our bearing on the top of the rise, running slower and slower, hearts thumping now; we had been walking all day since first light on nothing but glucose sweets and water; we were pretty fit, but it was a very bad stage of the very long, hot day to be running up a long, bad, hot hill in the hot dry sun after a rhino you were getting pretty sick of in a piece of country you had got very sick of towards the Portuguese border of Mozambique that went on for bloody ever. We ran, straggling, up the hill, and there over the top were the brown hills and valleys of Africa going on hot and dry and merciless for ever in the hot gold latening sun, on into the hazy mauve of Mozambique. Down there was the Ruya again, winding thin and rocky towards the mauve on its long way down to the Zambesi. And down there just two miles away as the crow flies the Ruya became the Luia, the invisible border.

'Find it!'

We were all looking, panting and sweating. Most probably he would head down to the Ruya to drink at this time, his spoor had not been near water all day and he would be thirsty now. He had not seen us when he disappeared over the hill so he would probably head for the nearest water now.

'Find it!'

Thompson found it, he slapped his hip and made off down the hill. He was heading for the river all right; the trouble was which part of the river, that called Ruya or that called Luia? There were only two hours of daylight left. He was probably running and we had to walk. The only chance was that he would rest by the river. This was his own territory. Thompson slapped his hip, calling Graham Hall. He pointed, panting, red-faced, sweating.

'Follow the spoor. I'll make a swoop downriver and try to cut him off and turn him back into Rhodesia. If you get a shot at him and you hit shout *Hit Hit* and I'll do the same.'

Thompson set off down the hill away from the line of spoor, and I ran after him. It was a bad thing to run now, but he was probably already at the Ruya, in which case he would not hear us and it was the only way to head him off from Mozambique.

We ran as quietly as we could looking for the hard ground, and across the ravine and up the next hill and I figured this must be the last Rhodesian hill, the other side would be Mozambique, we could not see the beacon from down here. We ran panting and heart-thudding up the hill, and I was nearly finished, then Thompson swung away to the west, across the hill, jogging. Then he waved me down behind him, and we walked towards the Ruya, panting, crouched a little.

We were maybe a quarter of a mile from the river now but we could not see it through the trees and grass. Thompson tested the wind with the ash-bag, panting. It was all right. We crouched across the hill, trying not to make any noise, walking, all the time trying not to pant out loud. The wind stayed with us. We covered four hundred yards and then we saw the river, eighty, maybe a hundred yards ahead, and we crouched down. We surveyed the banks and bush carefully, but we could see neither Graham Hall nor the beast. Thompson tested the wind with the ash-bag, then he started towards the river, very carefully.

Anything could happen, and maybe nothing. Maybe he was somewhere down there in the bush resting or feeding or watering or lying in the mud that maybe made him white, maybe he was already gone. Maybe across the Ruya and back up into the Rhodesian hills, or maybe straight down the river across the invisible line, gone into the hot brown-mauve of Mozambique, running, running from the place where he knew there were no more rhino. We crept slowly, carefully, down the slope towards the Ruya, and all the way we were marking out trees to go for if he broke cover. We could see or hear no sign of Graham Hall and the trackers. We had good vision upriver, maybe a hundred and fifty yards. Downriver we had even better vision, into Mozambique. Perhaps we were three hundred yards from the border, where the Ruya ran through the hills. Thompson tested the wind and it was well in our personal favour, going downriver towards Mozambique, but if the animal was upriver he would get Hall's wind, and he would break our way towards Mozambique, so the wind was not good. It would have been much better the other way round. We went very quietly and carefully, we were seventy yards from the river now, then sixty, then fifty. When we were maybe fifty yards from the river the bull broke cover.

He must have caught wind of Hall and suddenly he broke cover two hundred yards upriver. First there was the noise of his coming, the crashing and the huffing and the sound of him on the earth, then he came crashing out of the riverine bush into the open and he was going flat out, head up, ears back, tail curled, he was frightened, not just startled, and he was going flat out and he was heading straight down river towards us and Mozambique, running flat out, precisely where we didn't want him to go, Thompson had been dead right and he did the only thing possible to turn him. It was a dangerous thing to do and as he suddenly jumped up and ran, his blond head looked very significantly blond suddenly leaping up in the sun; he jumped up and ran through the trees towards the river straight at the beast's line of flight, like a rugby full-back and, as he ran, he bellowed and waved his gun, he bellowed, '*Aaarrh!*' and anything that came into his head to show himself to the beast and frighten it and make it swerve away from Mozambique and the beast came thundering, then it saw him and turned on him. The beast turned and came thundering straight at him, flat out, great grey-white, two-thousand-pound, armed beast, pounding, red-eyed, straight at him and Mozambique. It was no good, and Thompson leapt for the trees. He swerved and leapt at the last safe moment and scrambled up the tree, and the beast thundered at him. The beast thundered at the tree and gave a great swipe up at Thompson with his horn as he passed, then he thundered straight on.

I was also up a tree. It was a good tree, built like a stepladder and it gave a good view. The big grey-white beast, the last rhino in the Ruya, ran snorting and thundering, ears back, tail curled up, flat out, terrified, on downriver, heading for between the two hills. There he went. I watched him from my tree, running, running, I could see him for a long way, he went running, crashing, thundering, down alongside the Ruya, getting smaller and smaller, and now only glimpses between the trees, big grey black and haunches crashing through the grass between the hills, heading for the mauve between the two hills where the Ruya became the Luia. There he went. Then he was gone.

I climbed down out of my tree and I was very glad the Ruya was all over. I dropped down to the ground, and I watched Thompson climbing down and I thought: so it's not going to be Thompson who gets it. Coetsee was taking over tomorrow, in Mususumoya and then in the Gokwe, and by the time his month in charge of Operation Rhino was up the big rains would have come.

'Was he albino?' I said.

'I don't know,' Thompson said.

CHAPTER TWENTY-TWO

IT was late when we got back into Old Norman's camp, from the Mozambique border. We had covered maybe thirty miles that last day, following the big white bull, and we had not eaten and we were very tired. There were two more big fires in Old Norman's camp and a lot of natives sitting round them and two more Land-Rovers and two more tents. The Land-Rovers were British South Africa Police vehicles and there was a section officer and two patrol officers and half a dozen African constables and an African sergeant-major. There were maybe a hundred Africans standing and sitting round the two big fires, and thirty-five of them were handcuffed. They were the poachers. The rest were Old Norman's labourers and witnesses. There were two typewriters set up on camp-tables at the entrance to the police tents and Tilly lamps burning and the two European policemen were tapping away on the typewriters and there was an African constable sitting opposite them interpreting and a witness standing, making his statement. Old Norman was sitting at his camp-table outside his tent with a pile of documents and he was also interviewing witnesses. There was a big murmur of voices. Only Thompson knew that Old Norman was going to knock over the poachers today, we were all astonished to see the activity in Old Norman's unexpectedly big camp. Our porters were saying, 'Ah! ah! ma Polisa!' as we walked into Old Norman's camp, they were very impressed, staring, and the rest of us were grinning. God, it looked very good to see those thirty-five swines in handcuffs sitting there by the fire looking very worried, and the cops. Thompson was grinning all over his face.

'Congratulations!' He strode through the camp, hand outstretched to Old Norman. Old Norman looked up over his rimless spectacles, peering through the glare of his Tilly lamp, he had not heard us come in with all the noise in his camp.

'It was a hang of a lucky day,' he said.

'Congratulations, Old Norman.'

'Thanks, thanks,' Old Norman grinned quietly, fiddling with his spectacles. 'It was a hang of a successful day.'

Thompson beamed round delighted, hands on hips, at the thirty-five sons of bitches sitting round the fire. 'Bloody beautiful.'

'Look at this,' Old Norman said quietly, delighted with himself. We followed, delighted with him. There in the Tilly lamplight outside the police tent was a large selection of weapons, neatly laid out in rows on a groundsheet and labelled.

'Bloody marvellous!' Thompson said. 'Bloody excellent!'

There were nine firearms. There were three .303s, two of them looked in very good condition. There was one .93 and five old muzzle-loaders. They were all highly polished. Next to each weapon was neatly laid out the ammunition found with each gun. Next to each muzzle-loader was a selection of nails, ball-bearings, nuts, bolts, a few pot-legs. They were slugs for the old guns. There were packets of pouches and tins and bottles of gunpowder for the charges. 'Bloody marvellous!' Thompson grinned. We were all grinning.

'This muzzle-loader was made in seventeen hundred and something,' Old Norman picked it up. We examined it. It was a fine old weapon with a beautifully carved stock.

'You pack the gunpowder in here,' Norman indicated the small funnel next to the hammer, 'as a detonator, then you pour some more as a charge down the muzzle, then you pour some nails and nuts and bolts on top of that. Then you tamp it down with grass or something, then – *boom*.'

There was meant to be a flint which the hammer sparked off which ignited the detonator charge which set off the powder in the barrel, but the poachers could not get flints. So they had to ignite the powder with a match. Ignite the powder, take aim at the animal, hold the aim for anything up to a minute while the detonator charge fizzes, then *boom*. And clouds of smoke. Anything could happen. Many a man has blown himself up with a muzzle-loader.

'Bloody *excellent*!'

'Are they all in working order?'

'All,' Old Norman said.

I picked up another one. It was home-made. A steel pipe fixed on to a block of wood for a stock. 'Hell,' I said. There was no trigger but he had welded an elaborate affair together for a breach. 'I would hate to monkey round with this thing.'

'It takes a bit of nerve to fire a muzzle-loader,' Old Norman said.

You couldn't help admiring the swine who had the nerve to

have a go at an elephant or a buffalo or a rhino at close range with a sonofabitch of a gun like this, firing pot-legs and nails and bolts. The vicious turpitude lay in the fact that likely as not they only wounded the beast and it suffered agony and then turned rogue.

'*Bastards.*'

'What kind of gunpowder?' I said.

'All kinds,' Old Norman said, 'there's every kind there. Some of it's home-made out of fertilizers, some of it's made with the regular ingredients, some of it they've got out of cartridges, they get it from all over the place.'

'Bloody *excellent*, Norman,' Thompson said.

'Let's fire one,' I said.

'Okay,' Thompson said, delighted with life, 'you hold it.'

'No,' I said, 'you hold it.'

Next to the firearms was a bow and many arrows. The bow was well made. The arrows were fletched with chicken feathers and the heads were made out of sharpened bits of iron. Wrapped behind the heads was wadding to hold the poison.

'Absolutely bloody charming.'

And next to the bows and arrows, spread on a separate tarpaulin was a great mass of snares. Two game scouts were disentangling them and sorting them into piles. The game scouts grinned at us. There were seventy or eighty big snares there, made of three-eights of an inch steel cable, old mining cable, all rusty. The rust was deliberate, to disguise the shiny steel, and it was effected when the cable was heated to reduce its springiness. Some of the cables were lashed to stout logs, nine or ten feet long, which the snared beast dragged, to strangle it and leave an easy trail for the poacher to track. There were over three hundred guinea-fowl snares, made out of twisted baobab bark.

'*Very good work,*' Thompson beamed at the game scouts.

They beamed. 'Thanks, sah,' they beamed.

'*Bloody good work!*'

143

'And here,' Old Norman said. He led us to the next police tent. There were rows of hides laid out on the ground. There were at least ten kudu hides there and one elephant and I saw one lion and one leopard and there was one rhino horn and many bits and pieces of hide. They were all labelled. Thompson crouched down to examine them. 'And that's only a *fraction* of what they've taken.' There was a big pile of dried meat being sorted out by game scouts. There must have been a couple of hundred pounds of meat there.

'Drying on racks it was.'

'*Only a fraction.*'

'Where's the rest disappeared to?' I said.

'I know,' Old Norman said, 'I know. Just give me time.'

'Europeans?' I said.

'You'd be very surprised,' Old Norman said. 'And it doesn't stop in Rhodesia. Just give me time.'

'Just give our Old Norman *time*.' Thompson slapped him on the shoulder, delighted with him.

'Did any of them put up a fight?'

'No,' Old Norman said. 'They were so astonished. We caught the one that snared the cow which the vet came and operated on, he confessed.'

'*Did you now?*' Thompson's eyebrows went up.

'Over here.' Old Norman led the way to the big fire where all the natives were sitting. They were all staring. Two labourers were cooking up Government porridge in five big cooking pots. The thirty-five accused stared at us, firelight flickering on their black faces. Thompson glared at them, hands on hips.

'Which one?'

'There,' Old Norman pointed. The man lowered his eyes when we looked at him.

'Hey-*hey*!' Thompson glared at him malevolently across the firelight. The man shifted. Thompson glared at him: '*Why did you not follow up the cow and kill her?*'

The man lowered his eyes and said nothing.

'Do you know how deep that cable went? It went right down into the bone of her leg! For many months she could not walk properly, and she certainly could not run. It would have been very easy to follow and kill her! But you did not. Why?'

The man said nothing.

'Because you were too lazy!' Thompson shouted. 'Because it was too much trouble! You left the animal to suffer agony just to save yourself some trouble!'

Thompson glared at him. He wanted to shout a hell of a lot more, tell the cold-blooded sonofabitch what he would like to do to *him*, snare *him* round his bloody leg right down to the bloody bone and leave *him* to suffer. And a lot of other things. But he dared not say too much, until the magistrate had dealt with them.

'You cruel, cold-blooded sonofabitch.'

Old Norman pointed them out one by one, telling us about them. That one was a witch-doctor. He came to the Ruya every dry season to snare. He also did business, putting the *mushonga* on the other poachers' snares to bring them luck. He was also a rain-maker. He was a big wheel in the Ruya. None of the locals would testify against him, because he was a witch-doctor but that was all right, Old Norman had caught him red-handed. This one was also a gunsmith. He fixed everybody's guns for them. It was big business. But Old Norman standing there in the firelight in his spectacles was on to more than just these sonsabitches. They had given him a lot of information about the big boys behind them, the wholesale bastards, and they were the swines he was after now. Just give him time.

'Heh-hey,' Thompson said standing there, delighted, malevolent, hands on hips. 'Don't they look bloody *marvellous*?'

They looked very good all sitting there round the fire, all thirty-five of them good and handcuffed to each other and very worried, they looked very good indeed. And the police Land-Rovers and tents and the police uniforms and the typewriters going and the hundreds of snares all laid out on the tarpaulins

and the firearms and all the other exhibits, and all the witnesses and all Chief Masoso's people who had come to stand and stare in the big firelight in the late night in the middle of the African bush, it all looked very good and satisfying and impressive indeed.

That was our last night in the Ruya, and we had got over the frustration of the big white bull.

Part Five

CHAPTER TWENTY-THREE

BEFORE dawn the next morning Thompson shouted, '*Wake up – Vuka – Wake up!*' and we heaved ourselves out of our camp beds, not sorry at all that this was going to be the last time. We carried our lanterns up through the long grass to the stockade to start the last crating of the last three animals, to transport them to Gona-re-Zhou. It was cold and dark and the lamps shone bright yellow on the long grass and stout stockade and the animals huffed and puffed and charged in their pens as we approached, but when we climbed up the stockade and the lights shone bright yellow down on them standing there, big and grey and dangerous in the dry dust, they were mostly quiet, confused by the glare, the pressure lamps making their soft hissing noises. Brightspark Tafurandika brought me a mug of coffee up to the stockade, stumbling in the dark grass and slopping the coffee and looking as if he had had a gutsful of this rhino capture crack-of-dawn business. I told him to start breaking camp, to take down my tents and pack everything in my vehicle and when the sun came up to fry up some eggs and pancakes and a can of sausages. Thompson's cookboy brought him a mug of coffee and all the tents were coming down in the early morning moonlight. Everybody was still looking very sleepy. Mkondo and the Irvin and Johnson driver were reversing their great vehicles with the rhino crates on the back up to

147

the stockade, headlights lighting up the bush and their big diesel engines revving.

On the north side of the square stockade the earth was dug out, to make a long sloping pit the length of it, and the lorries with their crates reversed down into it and backed up to the stockade so their backs were at ground level of the stockade. The crates were made of very stout timber reinforced with strong steel bands and locking devices, each crate cost three hundred pounds. They were twelve feet long and eight feet high and four feet wide so that once the beast was in he could not turn around. The end where the head would be was sloped forwards so that when the rhino tried to smash his way out his horn would find no purchase and would slide up. The first crates had been vertical at both ends and by the time they got a few miles down the road the rhinos had their heads sticking out the smashed end. There were two short passages, jutting out from the side of the stockade, just wide and long enough to hold an adult rhino, and when the lorries were in position the labourers heaved the big heavy crates off the lorries and dragged them up to the open mouths of the two passages, much shouting and chanting and heaving. It was dawn when the crates were in position and then Thompson practised closing the crates.

The crate's big door was opened up into the passage and a long stout rope was tied to it and twenty labourers were put on to the rope.

'Are you ready?' Thompson shouted.

The twenty labourers were strung out far behind the crate like a tug-of-war team.

'*Don-sa!*' Thompson shouted and the natives heaved on the rope and the big swing door shut with a big bang.

'No, no, *no!*' Thompson shouted. 'You pull the rope like old women! How many times have we put the chipimbiri in the crate and yet you pull like old women! By the time you have closed the door like old women the chipimbiri has kicked it

148

open again and then he is frightened and will not enter the crate again!' He glared at them. 'You old women.'

They grinned, white teeth in the yellow lamplight dawn. They were probably glad to see the back of us too. They were only here for the beer. Thompson swung the big door open with disgust. 'Again.'

'Donsa!' and they heaved-ran-scrambled backwards with all their might and the door slammed shut with a big bang and they held it slammed, tugging on the tope. Thompson slammed the bolt home. He turned to them.

'Correct! Why is it that you only do it right after I have shouted at you? Enza, co-operate! Ah!'

After the practice we knocked off for breakfast. The sun was just coming up. I walked back to my camp and it looked very naked and disorganized and regretful with the tents all down and the things all over the place, with Brightspark Tafurandika trying to figure out a system. He had set the camp table and chair at the fireside with my breakfast and I sat down and ate it, looking at everything. It felt good next to the fire, warming my cold legs, the table in the sunrise, and it felt pretty sad, now that we were really going. We had had a good time in the Ruya and we had caught many chipimbiri and it felt very good each time and I had always been glad to come back to this camp at night, even to old Brightspark Tafurandika.

'Are you glad that we are going, Old-Fish-That-Does-Not-Drink?'

'Ah,' Brightspark Tafurandika said, 'I am very sad. And we have caught many chipimbiri.'

'*Who* has?' I said.

'*We* have,' Brightspark Tafurandika said toothlessly. 'Even army cooks are still soldiers.'

'Any army marches on its stomach?' I said to Brightspark Tafurandika, the most conscientiously underworked campcook in the business.

149

'Nkosi,' Brightspark Tafurandika said, 'how many chip-imbiri did you personally catch?'

'Okay, Brightspark,' I said. 'Where did you get that name from?'

'My mother,' Brightspark Tafurandika said.

'Mother love is a wonderful thing,' I said.

After breakfast I went back to the stockade. The sun was up now. I was the first, and the rhino snorted and huffed and charged at me through the gaps in the mopani poles when they saw me coming and their dust rose up, especially the cow called Barbara. I told her to shut up and she backed off and crashed at me again through the poles. Barbara didn't like *any*body. I climbed up the stockade and looked down at them. When they saw you up there and knew there was nothing they could do about it they gave up huffing and started chomping up a branch or something or had a go at each other through the gaps in the poles, especially Barbara. Sometimes they even looked as if they were enjoying your company in a limited sort of way, seeing they could not get at you to kill you, they would prob-ably be sorry if you climbed down and went away. I climbed along the top of the stockade to the centre where I could see down into all four pens and they all had a snort and a charge at me as I climbed along, especially Barbara, pounding across the pen then skidding to a stop on huge hooves so the dust clouded up and snorted and hooked up at my feet with their horns, but I was just out of reach and they knew it. I looked down at them one after the other standing down there, great and grey, as tall as a man at their shoulder, with their great horned heads and their piggy ears. They were bored and as they could not kill me they were quite pleased I was there, I was something to think about. They glared at me half-heartedly, hoping I would fall or do something interesting like that. The bull called Oswald started chomping a big, spiky piece of cactus thoughtfully, inch-long thorns and all, head up a little and stuck out a little and the piece of cactus sticking out of the side of his big mouth

like a cigar, as long and thick as a man's leg, and the white juice
dribbling down his chin, working the cactus in with his prehensile, meditative lip, watching me. Rhinos are very fond of
cactus, a rhino will give his right foreleg for a nice piece of
thorny cactus; the natives say that rhinos get drunk from eating
cactus, but Oswald was just chomping it for something to do.
In the pen next door the big cow who had been running with
the white bull was just standing around and the calf shuffled
around her looking very bored indeed and whimpering at her,
grizzling and being a pest. He looked up at me without enthusi-
asm and miaowed off elsewhere. He was maybe twenty months
old and his horn was a black rounded stump and the tissue
where it protruded was sort of rough and ragged. His ears had
scabs of blood and dust where he had been earmarked and they
still looked a little sore. He shuffled round the pen looking for
something to do, then he decided to have a suck, which was at
least something to do, and he went for her great loins and got
down on to his knees and his head disappeared half-heartedly
and his backside stuck up out. The cow just stood there. Barbara stood there watching me balefully, hoping without much
optimism for something to happen. As soon as I turned my
head in her direction she charged, head down, hooves scrambling the dust up, snorting, and she crashed her horn into the
poles I was standing on so that they shook. Then she backed off.
She looked at me with disgust, looked around hopefully, found
nothing so put her ears back bored, then worked herself up into
a rage and charged and crashed the poles again. She crashed the
mopani poles about a bit, then, having failed to provoke me, she
snorted at Oswald through the poles and lashed her horn about
at him. Oswald just stood there, munching his cactus. Barbara
backed off murderously, had a think, then charged at the cow
and calf through the other poles and smashed those around a
bit. The cow and calf took no notice whatsoever. I leant down
into the empty pen and pulled up a branch of feed that had
optimistically been placed there for the last white bull yester-

day, and I held it down to Barbara for her to eat. She thundered at it joyfully murderous and smashed it about with her horn. I pulled it out and she backed off. She eyed me malevolently, just waiting for me to try that again. I threw it down for her to eat and she crashed across the pen, horn down, red-eyed, and killed the branch dead. Then Oswald got fed up with his cactus, spat out the rest and made a few charges at Barbara who was having another go at killing the branch next door. Barbara was delighted; she turned from the branch lying there murdered and thundered at Oswald. They had a good go at each other through the poles, two two-thousand-pound beasts smashing at the big timbers to get at each other. The dust billowed up, and there was great snorting and pounding and crashing and eyes rolling red. Suddenly there was a dull snap and Barbara's horn was clean gone and there was just the big, red, round, raw bleeding place where it had grown and there was the horn lying in dirt under her thundering hooves. She did not falter, she thrashed the big rugged mopani timbers with her raw bloody nose trying to get at Oswald, then she backed off and then dropped her head and charged again and Oswald thundered and smashed on the other side; she backed off in a hurry and charged and smashed her bloody nose around again and again and the poles were wet, red with blood. They were having a good time but I grabbed another branch out of the empty pen and shouted and thrashed it at her to make her stop crashing the poles with her big raw snout; I shouted and beat the branch against the poles, and she turned on the branch. She charged it furiously and smashed up at the branch with all her rage. Oswald was still thrashing the other side of the poles, and I thrashed the branch at Barbara to keep her mind off Oswald whom she wanted to kill so badly and she thrashed the branch and the leaves were all bloody. Then Oswald got fed up and turned around and went back to his cactus disconsolately. Barbara continued to kill the branch a bit more, getting more and more half-hearted, then she lost interest. The horn has no nerve, it is just an agglutinated mass of compact fibre, but the raw base must have been sore. She looked back at Oswald hopefully, charged him again, smashed her nose again. I thrashed the branch again and she spun around, had another short go at killing it again, then she lost interest altogether. She stuck out her big prehensile lip like a finger and took a mouthful of the branch, snapped it off and chomped it moodily in the sunrise.

Then Thompson arrived and she had another go at smashing the poles down to get at him. When the labourers arrived she had a lovely bloody time trying to kill all of them. Oswald was chomping his cactus with overall disgust.

CHAPTER TWENTY-FOUR

FIRST, Thompson decided to get rid of Barbara because she was such a bloody nuisance, trying to kill everybody and smashing her nose up on the timber. Getting rid of Barbara was like taking candy from a kid.

The row of labourers were ready on the long rope lashed to the big open crate door. The game scouts began to pull out the poles of that part of her pen adjoining the passage and this drove Barbara crazy, she charged the poles and pounded them with her two thousand pounds and bloody nose, loosing them up nicely. As the gap widened she got madder and madder, attacking it, thrashing her wild bloody head, lunging through the gap, huge legs scrambling in the dust, heaving and thrashing wild-eyed and murderous to get at the crate she could see, to kill it. She could not force herself through the gap yet, she scrambled back furiously and charged again, joyously murderous, and the game scouts heaved up another pole and she hurled her wild head and shoulders through the gap but her big belly

could not get through yet. She roared with frustrated murderous intent, great forefeet scrambling, heaved herself back out,
the game scouts heaved another pole out each and Barbara
roared and charged again, head down, so the pen shook. She
fought and thrashed, squeezing through the gap, squealing in
rage, she burst through and in one wicked, murder-bend, roaring bound she charged at the offensive crate. Down the short
passage, straight into the crate to murder it and Thompson
shouted, *'Donsa!'* and the natives heaved and slammed the
big door behind her and Thompson slammed the bolts home.
It was like taking candy from a kid.

Barbara was pounding the sloped end inside the crate and
her big, bloody, hornless nose skidded up it, she squealed in
impotent rage and pounded and skidded and pounded and ski-
ded blood everywhere and then she tried to scramble up it, her
big bloody head lunged up at the ventilation opening in the top
of the crate and the blood flew, then she backed off to charge it
and found the door closed and she found she could not turn
round and then she really kicked and screamed and thrashed
and pounded and skidded. The big crate shook and banged and
thudded and squealed; we had a cigarette while we waited for
her to burn herself out some. Eventually she exhausted herself.
Only great wheezing panting came from inside the crate. It was
pretty bloody in there. Then Thompson leant down in through
the rear ventilation gap with a big syringe and rammed it into
her before she could kick and scream and pumped a dose of
morphine into her, for the pain in her nose. Then we
heaved and rolled and crow-barred and shoved and sweated
and cursed and shouted Barbara's crate back on to the Isuzu
lorry.

Oswald was very different to Barbara. He huffed and Puffed
and charged the poles as we were pulling them out, but when
they were out he investigated the situation very cautiously. He
sniffed about the opening and he did not like the look of it. We

154

were all dead quiet on the top of the stockade, watching, not daring to move to distract him. He sniffed cautiously through the opening, head down, alert, he made several false starts and backed out each time, then he ventured right into the passage sniffing and jerking ready to scramble back. Then he investigated the open crate. He advanced and retreated and advanced several times making big, dangerous, sniffing, snuffling noises, glaring into the crate, and we were all dead still; he advanced half a step at a time great legs and haunches tense, trembling, ready to scramble; he got half-way into the crate, then three-quarters in and only his haunches were out and Thompson had his hand up ready to signal *Donsa*, and Oswald got cold feet. He scrambled back out, huffing and puffing and snorting, looked around wild-eyed and then got stuck into the offensive crate door. He lunged at the big steel hinge and smashed at it with all his might, squealing his rage, so the crate shook. Then he spun around and lumbered back down the passage and through the gap back into his pen.

'Come on, you stupid old bastard.'

He glared at us.

'Come on.'

He just glared.

'Come on, you bloody idiot.'

Oswald just stood there.

'All right,' Thompson said. 'Sacks.'

Graham Hall dangled a sack down through the forward ventilation hole of the crate, Thompson dangled a sack into the passage at the gap. He flapped it.

'*Hey toro!*'

More than rhino flesh and blood could stand. Oswald thundered furiously at the sack to kill it, crashed through the gap, lunging, and Thompson whipped the sack up out of the way. '*Hey toro!*' Graham Hall shouted and flapped his sack down inside the crate and Oswald thundered headlong, murderous, into the crate to kill the sack and Thompson shouted, '*Donsa!*'

and the natives heaved the big door slammed shut and Thompson slammed the bolt home.

'Ole,' he said.

Then we started on the cow and calf. They took a long time, and a lot of sweat and cursing. We had to lasso the calf, which took a long time and a lot of cursing because nobody could throw a lasso like a cowboy. After a long time and a lot of cursing and advice and counter-advice we managed to drop a noose round the calf's neck. Then we opened the pen for the cow to go through and we shouted at her and flapped the sacks at her and goaded her, but she wasn't going anywhere without the calf and we could not let the calf go with her because no crate was big enough for two. In the end we had to shoot a dart of M99 into her. Then we had to lasso her too, before she went down, and to get her to a different crate we led the rope through the gap in the fence into Barbara's old pen, then through the other gap, down the passage and through the length of the crate and out of the forward ventilation hole and then everybody heaved on the rope. We had to drag her through all the gaps into the passage before she went down under the M99, and though she could not fight much on account of the drug she still knew she did not want to go anywhere. She dug in her great four feet and heaved back, wheezing and gasping against the big rope, great, bulging neck stuck out and mouth open, groaning, and her wild eyes drunk, and it was like trying to drag the Albert Hall. It took a long time, cursing and shouting and sweating, a few feet each time, to get her into the crate. And the calf thrashed against his rope, trying to follow her. Then we dragged him into his crate.

He squealed all the way, fighting, and when we finally got him into his crate he cried for his mother.

Then we heaved the crates on to the lorries and lashed them down. We set off straight away in convoy for Gona-re-Zhou, the Irvin and Johnson lorry and the Isuzu lorry and the Volkswagen escort vehicle. The rest of the camp would leave later in the day for Mususumoya. It was seven hundred miles from Nyamasota to Gona-re-Zhou and we had to drive non-stop because the beasts had no water in their crates.

CHAPTER TWENTY-FIVE

WE drove in convoy through the hot dry bush, bouncing and jolting and throwing up the big trails of dust, Nevin and I in front in the escort Volkswagen truck, then the Irvin and Johnson vehicle, then the Isuzu, a mile apart so we did not chew each other's dust. We were averaging fifteen miles an hour, so as not to throw the rhino about too much. They would all be lying down in their crates because they felt unsafe on their feet. I wondered what they thought was happening to them. Everything, so far, must have been comprehensible to them, the hunt, the captivity, the people, the smells and sounds, even the manhandling into the crates; but the dark crates, the confinement so they could not turn round, the engines, and the movement and the jolting were totally outside their comprehension. They would be very frightened, but there was no other way of doing it. There were several tracks leading from the Nyamasota area winding through the bush to Mount Darwin, and we were following the longest route because it was the best. It was very boring and tedious jolting along at fifteen miles an hour, the Volkswagen could have gone much faster but we had to keep pace with the lorries in case something went wrong. We had a roger-roger in the Volkswagen to radio for help. We had a multibox. Cigarettes. I even had a few warm beers.

The dust churned up high and thick and opaque and choking behind us and it hung and it swirled in through the open windows. The earth was crying out for rain but it would not rain for another month, till the hottest month, October, suicide month. We crossed the Bungwe and the Mudzi and the Shamba, down into the river-beds and grinding up the other side and you wondered that there had ever, even once upon a time, been water in them, and you thought *fifteen bloody miles a bloody hour*. Escort duty was unpopular.

From the top of the hills the yellow-brown-grey bush turned misty mauve in the heat. Sometimes there were ploughed fields, waiting hard and brown for the rain, and the cattle we saw were thin. When there were fields you could usually see the kraal of the men who owned the fields, pole and dagga huts and ragged thatch and a few little pole and dagga grain huts and a cattle pen made of brushwood and two or three wives depending on how wealthy he was and a lot of snotty-nosed children and skinny dogs and chickens scratching and some goats and maybe a few runt pigs. There were many goats. The goats are no good for eating and they eat up all the grazing; a man would do much better to keep sheep or more pigs, but it is impossible to persuade a man to get rid of his goats, because he likes to count his goats. Goats make him feel wealthy, you buy wives with goats and cattle. The more goats you have the more wives, the more children, the more daughters to sell as brides for more goats. It stands to reason. The people in the kraals always waved staring as we drove by at fifteen miles an hour, maybe twenty-five for a bit then slowing down again, and the children ran out skipping and grinning and jumping excitedly. Sometimes there was a signpost nailed to a tree. Sometimes we stopped to give the lorries a chance to catch up. We let them overtake us, great clouds of dust and the big, black rhino crates jolting passed, then we overtook them again. We were covered in fine dust, eyebrows, teeth, the corners of our mouths. We kept our bush hats on to keep most of it out of our hair.

'Fifbloodyteen miles a bloody hour.'

When we passed the signpost to the Mary Mount Mission

and Clinic there was a native bus churning along the road, and with the signpost and the bus and all it seemed like a Woolworths on a Saturday morning. A long time after that we came to Nyamahoboko, which is three native stores for no apparent reason. All in a row, corrugated iron roofs and cement steps, hot under the sun in the middle of the bush. One had a big Coca-Cola sign and the other had a big Hubbly-Bubbly sign and the other had a very big red-and-white poster across one wall reading, *Top The Action With Life Cigarettes*. There were some chickens and some natives sitting in the sun. They stared at us. We stopped to give the lorries a chance to catch up and I went into the store with the Hubbly-Bubbly sign, owned by S. N. Zichawo, *Prop*. It smelt of sugar and calico and mealies and ropes and ploughshares and sweat.

'Give us a Hubbly-Bubbly,' I said.

Mr. S. N. Zichawo beamed apologetically.

'No Hubbly-Bubbly only Coca-Cola,' he beamed.

'What? No Hubbly-Bubbly?'

'No, sah.'

'But it says outside *Always Drink Hubbly-Bubbly It's Good For You*. Coca-Cola is next door.'

'Yes, sah.'

'Been a run on Hubbly-Bubbly in Nyamahoboko, has there?'

'Yes, sah,' Mr. S. N. Sichawo beamed.

'You should take down that sign,' I said. 'It misleads the travelling public. Got any beer?'

'Yes, sah,' Mr. S. N. Zichawo beamed. 'Lion beer or Castle beer, sah?'

'Not for me,' Nevin said, 'I'm on duty.'

'Okay,' I said, 'a Lion for me and Coca-Cola for the National Parks and Wildlife Management Department.'

The sun was getting low when we pulled into Mount Darwin. There is a joke about a Rhodesian town called Enkeldoorn, which means only-thorn, which goes: there is a national competition and the first prize is one week's holiday in

Enkeldoorn, the second prize is two weeks' holiday in Enkeldoorn, and so on, but that joke should be about Mount Darwin. Mount Darwin is too unimportant even to have a joke made about it. We pulled into the petrol station and the lorries trundled in behind us. While they were refuelling I climbed up on to the crates to see the rhino. They were all lying down, very docile and frightened, ears going. They knew I was clambering over their crates but they did not stand up to challenge me, or even look up, just lay there. Barbara looked very bad with her bloody nose and the blood smeared all over the timbers, just lying there. I was worried about how she would get on in the Gona-re-Zhou, without her armour. She still had her second horn to fight with, but it was short and far back on her head and it would not be very efficient, and she would take some time to get accustomed to using it. I wondered if the lions would notice that she had lost her main armour and I thought they probably would notice but they would probably leave her alone anyway. She would have to change her ways, stop trying to kill everybody, until her front horn grew again. The calf looked very miserable. With the engine stopped he could smell his mother again in the next crate and he was crying and she answered. But neither stood up. I asked the drivers how they had behaved and they said that at first they had kicked and screamed, then they had lain down. I wondered whether they were feeling carsick. There was a large crowd of Africans gathered round the lorries saying, 'Ah! ah!'

At the garage we washed the dust off our faces and arms. Then we stopped at the Greek Kaffir store to buy some beer, for me, for the long night journey. The beer was cold, the first cold beer we had seen for a long time and I wrapped it in newspaper. It was late afternoon and I thought, the rhinos must be getting thirsty now, sundown is their drinking time. It was impossible to give them water in their crates, they just attacked the buckets and smashed them up; it had been tried. They would not get a drink till we got to Gona-re-Zhou.

CHAPTER TWENTY-SIX

THE lorries could do forty miles an hour now, on the better road to Bindura and it felt very fast. The sun began to go down and the hard brown and yellow began to turn grey-mauve and the horizon was flaming red and orange and yellow, vast and silent; and then the bush began to turn dark but the west was still red and it was the best time in Africa, and I opened my first beer since Nyamahoboko and my first cold beer in a long time.

'What about the workers?' I said.

'I'd better not,' young Nevin said.

Outside Bindura we hit the tarmac. It was five minutes to six o'clock and we had to make a progress report to Head Office on the roger-roger. We pulled off on to the side of the road. The rhino lorries came roaring along and we waved them on and the drivers waved. The rhino crates looked very good thundering through the sunset on their long way to Gona-re-Zhou. We switched on the roger-roger, waiting for six o'clock and I opened another beer and Nevin permitted himself one swallow, just to kill the germs, and we listened to the Tsetse Fly Control officers reporting their day's tally to their Head Office, and it made very ugly listening indeed. The Tsetse Fly Control hunters are civil servants whose job it is to hunt out two wide corridors across Rhodesia, one in the north at the top of the Zambesi Escarpment, six hundred mile long, and one in the south-east, a hundred and twenty miles long. Altogether it is twenty-two thousand square miles of Rhodesia they have to hunt out, keep clear of game, kill, kill, kill within those corridors, kill the game to starve the cursed tsetse fly that brings the fatal sleeping sickness to man and the nagana to cattle, the dread unicellular corkscrew organisms called trypanosomes that bring the fever, then the sleeping sickness, then the wasting away, then death. The game carry the trypanosomes, the fly feeds on the game, then feeds off cattle and man and injects the trypanosomes into them. Maybe that is why Africa was called the dark continent, because in so much of it no man could use draft animals to explore it. Sleeping sickness, and the controlling of it is equally ugly. Kill the game to starve the fly. Very far away over the red and black horizons the tsetse fly boys were sitting at their Land-Rovers in the middle of their stretches of bush reporting to Head Office on their roger-rogers, taking it in turns.

'Number four thousand seven hundred and fifty-seven, one adult wart-hog, male.'

'Roger,' Head Office said.

'Number four thousand seven hundred and fifty-eight, one adult kudu, female.'

'Roger.'

Every year many many head of game is destroyed in the corridors. Each hunter with twenty-five African hunters under him, every dawn going out from their base camp, every night coming back to the European with the information of what they had shot, every night the reports to Head Office on the roger-roger. All right, it is necessary. It is the only way to hold the tsetse fly back behind the corridor, starve it, a scorched earth policy in the corridors which the tsetse cannot fly over. Every African country has to do it. If you did not have the corridors the fly would spread over the whole country and kill every man and domestic beast it found. If you did not have the corridors all the natives' cattle would die. If you did not have the corridors the whole native economy would be destroyed, and ours. If you did not have the corridors Africa would become the dark continent again. That might not be such a bad idea, at that. All right, they say it is the only way, and I believe them. But it did not make pretty listening on the radio.

It was late when we went through Salisbury and we stopped to refuel and we bought fish and chips for ourselves and the drivers, and some biscuits and some U.D.I. chocolate which is not bad stuff at all. The rhinos were still lying down and the calf called to its mother, and they looked pretty miserable. A policeman passed the filling station and he said, 'What have you got in those crates?' and I said, 'Rhinos,' and he said, 'There's no need to be funny.'

We drove through the night, a few miles apart, the Volkswagen in front and then the two big lorries, roaring along the tarmac at fifty miles an hour, headlights beaming, with the four big crates with the four great, unhappy beasts lying in them hearing the noise of the engines and the tyres. They must have been cold on the back of those lorries, fifty miles an hour through the night. And very thirsty. Very seldom did we see another vehicle and there were very few lights of farm homesteads. At midnight we went through Enkeldoorn, which is as good a time as any to go through Enkeldoorn. I tried to stay awake to keep Nevin company. There was nothing to do except think, and talk a little, and watch the African night go by, and cigarettes did not taste good any more. It was a very long night. Then we entered the lowveld, the sugar-cane country. It was dawn when we got to Triangle, and very still and beautiful. The rhinos looked very unhappy. At Buffalo Range we turned off the tar and headed down to the vast Gona-re-Zhou. We sent the Isuzu ahead, because the driver knew the way well, and we followed to guide the slower Irvin and Johnson vehicle. We had come six hundred miles from Nyamasota, and it felt like it, and I guess the rhino felt like it too.

CHAPTER TWENTY-SEVEN

IT was nine o'clock when we got into the Gona-re-Zhou, two thousand square miles of game reserve. It was much hotter, down here in the lowveld, and the trees were greener and from the hills you could see the side belt of lush dark green riverine vegetation along the banks of the wild, wide, winding Lundi river against the vast mauve of the bush that went on all the way to the horizon. The Lundi was low at this time of the year, but there was still plenty of water and the wide banks were of heavy white clean river-sand, like beaches, in places fifty-sixty yards wide before you got to the water, and the rocks were grey and hot and the big reeds that grew along the water's edge were very green; from the hilltop the Lundi was dark blue and when you got down to it the water was dark clear green also. There are many fish in the Lundi, bream and tiger-fish and vundu and even swordfish that come up from the far-away sea, and crocodile and many hippo, and all the game down there in the vast, silent Gona-re-Zhou. It was good natural rhinoceros country. We jolted slowly over the rough tracks, over the silent hills and down through the valleys, leading the big Irvin and Johnson lorry, heading for the place called Chipinda Pools, about eight miles from the Lundi. We passed a big herd of elephant feeding near the road. We stopped to watch them and they carried on feeding, stretching up their trunks and grabbing bunches of leaves, breaking them off and then curling up their trunks and stuffing them in their mouths. They were making a lot of noise, the breaking of the branches and the distant rumble of their stomachs. They were not worried about us watching them but two were keeping an eye on us while they fed. We saw three kudu and some hippo trails and three wart-hogs. Then we drove along a flat plain and then through a great glade with big trees, and there ahead was the stockade, the release point. There was the Isuzu, and the first thing we saw was that a rhino crate had fallen off the back. 'Oh God.'

The crate stood on end, leaning at an angle against the back of the lorry. There was Osborne, the Ranger in charge of Chipinda Pools sweating and cursing with his gang of Africans to get the crate back up on to the lorry.

'What happened?'

Osborne took off his sweat-stained hat and threw it on the ground. He was a big well-nourished, happy-faced, balding, perspiring, good-natured, exasperated man and he told us what had unprintably happened. Seems the unprintable ropes holding the unprintable crate had unprintably worked loose and when the Isuzu was unprintably reversing down into the unprintable pit with the sides lowered so the crate could be unprintably slid off up to the stockade, the driver had suddenly slammed on his unprintable brakes and simultaneously the rhino had unprintably kicked and the unprintable crate had crashed unprintably off. I looked at the up-ended crate.

'That's Barbara's crate,' I said.

'Whoever she is she's highly cheesed off.'

There was a loud crash and the crate shook. Barbara was sitting on her arse in there like a circus rhinoceros. Poor Barbara was having an eventful time with the National Parks and Wildlife Department. 'How long has she been like that?'

'Half an hour.'

There was another loud bang and scrambling and a loud protesting wail and the crate shook again. You could see her point of view. A lot of things had happened to her in the last forty-eight hours. '*Come on!*' Osborne shouted at his Africans.

He was trying to raise the crate back on to the lorry with a *wena-kamina*. A *wena-kamina* is a kind of block-and-tackle, made of steel, and two men work the block with a big lever

which they push to and fro between each other; *wena* means
'you' and *kamina* means 'me'. He had lashed the cable round
the bottom of the crate and the *wena-kamina* was lashed to a
big tree in front of the lorry, trying to heave the crate back up
on to the lorry and a gang of Africans were levering up under
the crate with short poles. '*Heave!*' Osborne shouted and we all
threw our grunting weight upwards on Barbara's crate and the
wena-kamina men pumped furiously on the handle and the big
crate creaked up an inch and the lorry springs creaked down
and Barbara kicked and screamed and the crate thumped back.
It was no good. It would take hours to get it back on to the lorry
so it could be driven up to the stockade.

'We'll have to forget it. We'll have to lower the crate all the
way and turn her loose without a drink.'

That was the purpose in transferring her first from the crate
into the stockade, to give her a drink. Once she was turned loose
she would have to find her own water and she had not had a
drink for over thirty-six hours.

'How far to the nearest water from here?'

'Eight miles. She'll find it, but it may take her some time.'

'How long?'

'A day. Because she's in strange country and she'll be
nervous.'

That was a bad pity. Rhinos have to have their drink. But she
could last a few days.

'She's broken her horn, she hasn't got any armour. So she'll
be very nervous in strange territory.'

'Barbara's too stupid to be frightened of anything,' Nevin
said.

'She'll smell the water,' Osborne said. He was a bit worried.
'It'll take her time but she'll get to it. I hope no other rhino
stops her crossing its territory.'

I wished she had not lost her armour. She was going to be
very fed up by the time she found her drink. I wondered how
sore her nose was. I climbed up on to the lorry and looked

carefully into the front ventilation hole of the up-ended crate. There she was, sitting on her great haunches like a dog begging and she glared at me wild-eyed, with murder in her heart. Big wheezing angry breathing. Her nose was bleeding afresh from the banging around in the crate. Barbara was up to here with the National Parks and Wildlife Management Department.

Osborne unlashed the *wena-kamina* and ordered an African to shin up a big tree with the cable and lead it up over a fork. Then he lashed the cable round the end of Barbara's crate. 'Wena-kamina!' he shouted. The two men started working the lever, 'Wena-kamina – wena – kamina.' The cable tightened half an inch each push. Then it took the strain and Barbara's up-end creaked another inch higher, off the edge of the back of the lorry. Barbara kicked and wailed and the crate shook. Then Osborne drove the big lorry out of the pit, out of the way.

'Okay,' he shouted to the *wena-kamina* men. 'Enza reverse.'

The big crate began to creak down again. Barbara thumped about again and the tree shook. We all moved well back, in case the high branch tore off down. That would have been very tough on Barbara. That would have been the very last bloody straw. She came down an inch at a time, thudding and crashing and shaking up the tree all the way. The big crate creaked down slowly, then it was level. Suddenly she stopped protesting. Just big wheezing, ominous breathing noises.

'Is she fed up with us.'

'Right,' Osborne shouted. He looked around. 'Everybody up trees. Mpofu!' He looked about for his game scout.

'Nkosi?'

'Drive my Land-Rover away, far far over *thereeeh*, enza good-bye.'

All the natives laughed. They were climbing up the stockade and trees. Nevin drove the Volkswagen away. He was very tired.

Osborne said to the Irvin and Johnson driver:

'Has your boss got plenty of money?'

'Yassah,' the Irvin and Johnson driver said, 'too much-i'

'All the same, he'd like his lorry back. Better move it.'

Osborne had set up a camp for the day a hundred yards away under the trees, it was the first time I had noticed it. The camp-table was set for his breakfast. 'Madara?' he shouted at his old cook.

'Mambo,' the old boy mumbled from somewhere.

'Do you want a rhino horn up your backside?'

'No, Mambo,' the old boy said.

'Then get up a tree.'

'Okay, Mambo. Mambo?'

'Yes?'

'What about your things?'

'If she interferes with my things,' Osborne shouted, 'I want you to shin rapidly down the tree and stick your finger in her eye.'

'Okay, Mambo.'

The Africans were festooned everywhere, up the stockade, up trees, grinning. I was up a good tree, in a fork.

'You all look beautiful,' Osborne said. 'You all look exactly right.'

He climbed up on top of the crate. Barbara was dead quiet. He lay down on top of the crate and hung down over the door and began to unscrew the big bolt with a monkey-wrench. We were all watching him. He unscrewed the bolt carefully, the nut came off. Then he eased the big bolt up out of the slot. Then he swung the big door open, and there stood Barbara's massive, grey, ominous hindquarters.

She just stood there. She could not tell that the door was open behind her.

'Hey,' Osborne said.

Barbara just stood there.

'Hey!' Osborne leant down and jabbed her with his finger.

Barbara snorted and came lumbering out backwards. She

168

came awkwardly, dangerously, lumbering out, massive hind-quarters first, then her big head appeared, snorting, and her bloody head was down and her piggy eyes were bloodshot with rage, and she took one swirling snort and then she got stuck in to the crate with Osborne clinging on top.

She threw her great self at the crate with all her two-thou-sand-pound outrage and belted it with her bloody stump, snort-ing, and the big crate rocked and Osborne clung on top shouting. '*Go awaaaay!*' She belted it and crashed it with all her might and the big crate rocked and skidded and bounced and banged and Osborne clung on yelling '*Go awaaaay!*' We were all laughing and it was a very good thing for Osborne that she did not have her front horn to get leverage with on the crate for she would have thrown Osborne, crate and all, over the Gona-re-Zhou; she crashed the crate murderously, then she looked around wildly for something more satisfying to kill. She saw the stockade and thundered at it, furious, hooves pounding, and crashed it with her bloody nose so the timbers shook and the natives hung on, she charged down the length of the stock-ade snorting and crashing it murderously; sore as a gumboil. She thundered round the end of the stockade looking for some-thing else to kill, then she saw Osborne's breakfast camp and that was it.

'*Hey!*' Osborne shouted. '*Hey!*'

Barbara was charging full two-thousand-pound tilt across the clearing at his nice breakfast camp.

'*Hey!*' Osborne yelled from the top of the crate, '*come back here!*' and Barbara paid no attention whatsoever, she thundered straight on the camp – '*Hey!*' Osborne screamed – and Barbara hit his camp. She hit it at full two-thousand-pound tilt joy-ously, smack, bang, crash she hit the folding camp-table and it flew high through the air, cart-wheeling cups and saucers and plates and cutlery flying all over the place. '*Hey!*' Osborne screamed jumping up and down on top of the crate, '*stop that at once!*' and Barbara hit the camp-chair and it flew over the treetops beautifully. '*Cut that out!*' Osborne screamed and there were loud bangs and crashes as Barbara was getting stuck into his pots and pans, pots and pans flying all over the place and we were all laughing and Osborne was screaming, '*MADARA!*'

'Nkosi?' from somewhere up in the trees above the crashing of the pots . . .

'*Stick your finger in her eye!*'

And the Africans screamed with laughter. She made a very impressive sight over there getting stuck into Osborne's pots and pans, head down, snorting, red-eyed crashing, pounding, pursuing them over the ground. We were all laughing. Then she had flattened the camp. She took one murderous snorting look around, then she spun around and went crashing off through the bush with black ingratitude into her new hinterland.

We watched her disappearing through the grass, the sun on her back. We were all laughing, and very impressed. She was heading in the wrong direction for water.

CHAPTER TWENTY-EIGHT

WE heaved and crow-barred and cursed the second crate which held Oswald off the lorry and up into the mouth of the stockade. Then Osborne got on top of the crate and unscrewed the big bolt. Oswald came thundering out in reverse, wild-eyed and turned and thundered into the pen, then skidded to a stop, dust flying. He glared around, outraged to find himself back at square one. He charged and crashed the mopani poles furiously. We encouraged him, shouting and waving at him while the game scouts thrust back the poles to seal off the pen. Then we stopped. Oswald carried on smashing up the pen a bit, then stopped, nonplussed at the silence. He looked around malevolently. There was a drinking hole for him but he was too mad with us to notice it. He wanted blood, not water.

'*Drink*.'

Oswald spun on my poles and charged them. I hung on. Then he looked around for anybody else, then he saw an offensive tree growing in the corner of the pen and he got stuck into that. Then he saw the water. He ran across the pen to the water, head down.

'Hooray.'

He stuck his nose into the water and began to slurp greedily.

First we released the calf into the adjoining pen, but he was too frightened of anything, the journey, the new air, the new pen, to notice the water. He just stood in the middle looking up at us, frightened and when we tried to show him where the water was by throwing things into it he just shied away. Then we dragged his crate away and brought his mother's crate up to the same pen. He could smell it was his mother and he ran up to the door and whimpered and the big cow kicked and crashed and answered. Osborne waved his arms to shoo him away and the calf charged at him and crashed the door with his stumpy horn and then big mommy inside kicked and the crate shook and Osborne had to clutch to keep his balance. '*Voetsak!*' he shouted at the calf and it charged and crashed the door again and Osborne clutched shouting, '*Voetsak!*' Finally he got the nut undone. As he swung the door open the calf ran headlong at his mother's massive hindquarters and tried to scramble head down ears back round them into the crate with her. She came backing out with a big bewildered snort and nearly trampled him underfoot. She came scrambling, blinking, furious, bewildered out, falling over her calf and then she whirled around and charged into the pen, and the calf galloped after her. She stood there bewildered, huffing and puffing, glaring at us.

'Now will you please *drink*?' She spun on Osborne and charged at the poles he was standing on and crashed them.

'Why me? Why always me?' We were all laughing.

I threw a stick down into the water so it splashed. She charged at the stick, then she saw the water. She sniffed it once ravenously and took one slurp to call the calf and nudged him with her hind-leg out from where he was trying to get at her teats, and he came hurrying to the water. He buried his nose straight in it thirstily and his mother turned around to glare at us while he drank. She was not taking any more chances. She glared at us angrily, great flanks heaving, head up. She must have been very thirsty but she was not going to turn her back on us with her calf around.

'All right,' Osborne said, 'everybody climb down off the stockade.'

He detailed one game scout to keep watch and tell us when she had drunk. We walked across to his flattened camp for breakfast. Madara had picked up most of the pieces.

The game scout called, as soon as we started eating:

'She has drunk.'

We finished eating. Osborne was happy again. I was not so tired, because I had slept a little in the Volkswagen, but Nevin was very tired. It was a beautiful Rhodesian day. We could hear the rhino in the pens. We ate the food off saucers because Barbara had flattened all Osborne's plates. The eggs were scrambled because Barbara had shaken their box up a bit in passing, but they were very good. I wondered how Barbara was getting on out there.

'I wish she had had a drink first,' Osborne said.

'Barbara'll be all right,' I said. 'She'll make friends everywhere.'

'I pity the bull who chats up Barbara.'

'She'll probably go all coy and girlish,' I said.

It was good down here in the Gona-re-Zhou, with Barbara somewhere out there finding her way, and all the other new rhino out there somewhere, and the three beasts now in the pens. In due course they would all find each other, in two years' time there would be many new calves. This was good rhino country. Once upon a time there used to be plenty here, but they had all been shot and snared out, before it was proclaimed a game reserve. It felt good to be here in the middle of a piece of two thousand square miles where it was all starting all over again.

'This time,' Osborne said to Madara, 'you will pack the remnants of my property in my Land-Rover and accompany it to a distant place of safety.'

We went back to the stockade and climbed up on it. The beasts huffed and puffed at us.

'Everybody had enough to drink?' Osborne inquired of them. 'Everybody happy?'

Oswald had a go at him, crashed the poles once, then backed off.

'Water,' Osborne informed them politely, 'is that way,' he pointed and Oswald had another go at his poles. 'Nourishment,' he waved his hand, 'grows on trees. Poachers are few, if any. Please address any complaints to the Senior Warden, not to me. Please do not kill each other too much. Please do not murder the hired help, particularly me. We hope you enjoy your stay. We look forward to seeing you again, at a considerable distance. Please do not call again. Good-bye,' he beamed at each of them in turn, 'good-bye. Let that idiot bull go first.'

Everybody was perched on top of the stockade and up trees. All the vehicles were reasonably far away. There was no property about except the water bowzer. The water bowzer was a steel cart that held a hundred and fifty gallons of water, which weighed three thousand pounds. Only a Sherman tank could hurt the water bowzer. The game scout started pulling out the poles of Oswald's pen, two at a time, and Oswald went mad.

He charged, furious, red-eyed, and smashed up at the poles and the fence shook and the poles leaped and jammed, he backed off thunderously and charged at the next poles that dared to move and smashed them, and the gap was almost big enough for him to get through; he flung his great self into it furiously, snorting, great hooves scrambling in the dust, he could not make it and he scrambled back enormously, dust flying, furious, and I was even worried about the water bowzer. The cow next door was placidly chewing a branch and her calf was suckling. The game scouts heaved at two more poles and Oswald came thundering. He crashed his shoulders through snorting and thrashing his horn and his big gut held him back, he gave a squealing snort of rage and thrashed his great legs and twisted and heaved and scrambled, and Oswald burst through the gap to freedom.

He burst through in a big scrambling, stumbling crash and he righted himself snorting, and the first thing he saw was the water bowzer, and he ran straight at it. He charged straight on at it snorting, then he swerved round it and he stopped. He looked back at us once, ears forward, then he turned around.

He went off into the strange bush at a demure trot. Making his huffing puffing noises. With his tail curled up over his back. Pretending that he knew exactly where he was heading.

The cow was still very quiet. She stood in the far corner of her pen, as far as possible from us, with the calf behind her. She was watching us, still chomping a branch. The calf's head was poking out behind her massive rear. They had not shown any greater interest or anxiety throughout the time Oswald had been drumming up his anticlimax. As long as it wasn't hap-pening to them.

The game scouts started on the poles, and the cow snorted and dropped her head and backed into the corner, bumping the calf behind her. But she was not going to charge. She was only huffing and puffing. She watched, dead still. The calf stuck his head out behind her and watched too, then put his ears back. The cow saw the gap, but she just watched it. Her flanks were heaving but she was not picking any fights. Two more poles came out and the gap was almost big enough for her to squeeze through but she just stood there, glowering. Then two more poles then two more. The gap was quite big enough for them now.

'Come on, madam.'

She huffed and glowered but she would not come on. She had her head down, but defensively. We waited for her. Then we all went dead quiet and did not move, standing along the top of the stockade. Then she came out of the corner, uncertainly.

Slowly, with her head down, smelling the ground so the dust puffed up a little, and her eyes were rolled forward, showing the whites, and the calf followed. She advanced, huffing cautiously, on the gap with the calf shuffling behind her, she looked through the gap with her eyes rolled forward taking big sniffs at the ground, then she went through uncertainly. The calf jostled through after her, she did not look up at us, nor left nor right. She broke into a small lumbering trot, as uncertain and cautious as can be, then she saw the water bowzer.

The first foreign thing she saw was the water bowzer and she dropped her head with a big snort and charged. She thundered straight at the big steel water bowzer, head down eyes red snorting, with the calf galloping behind her, '*Not my water bowzer*,' Osborne screamed, and she hit it. She hit the big steel three-thousand-pound water bowzer that only a Sherman tank could hurt sideways on at full thundering crashing gallop, and it flew like an empty can. She hit it with her great horned head in the undercarriage and swiped up with her great neck and the big cart flew up above her ten feet turning over in the air, water cascading everywhere, it hit the ground with a great watery crash and splash and Osborne was screaming, '*Leave my water bowzer!*' and she bounded, thundering snorting head down after it and she crashed the water bowzer again with all her rage and hooked it and it flew again even higher, cart-wheeling, wheels spinning, water spewing in all directions and it crashed in a big heap and the cow thundered after it. She crashed smack bang straight into it again horn first and crashed it along the ground, over and over through the grass, she thundered after it smashing it with her horn. It was very impressive. Then she crashed her horn between the spokes and she could not get it out and she gave a great roar of rage and threw her great furious head from side to side and the big water bowzer shook on the end of her horn, and then her horn snapped off half-way up and the water bowzer crashed free and inert and it was clearly dead. She gave it one last valedictory swipe with her broken stump, then she turned about panting and snorting and furious and glared about and collected her calf. She glared at us crouched up there on top of the stockade, then she came trotting enormously, dangerously, head up, ears forward, towards us with the calf trotting behind her.

She stopped half-way and glared at us, great flanks heaving, and we looked at her, very impressed and not saying anything, not even Osborne. Then she was satisfied that she had impressed us. She turned away with a huffing snort and set off rapidly at a big lumbering, flapping trot, and the calf cantered behind her, ears back, and we watched her go.

She lumbered off through the yellow grass at a trot, head up, broken horn up, ears forward, looking about her as she went, and the calf cantered behind her. The sun shone golden-grey on their backs above the grass and you could hear the big sound of her trotting. We still stood up on the stockade. She went maybe two hundred yards like that, then suddenly she stopped. She did not know where she was going. She turned around and looked back at us, head up, ears forward. Then she turned sideways on to us and looked in that direction, ears forward. She looked, then she turned around and looked in the opposite direction. We could not see the calf behind her. She was looking in all directions, smelling and feeling the new hinterland, and listening, her ears going all the time. She was smelling the land and listening for danger. Maybe she was also trying to smell out the water. She did not know which way to go for the best in this country. Then she made a decision, she turned and went off at her massive trot again. We still stood on top of the stockade, watching. She looked very good, setting out in the sunshine into the new hinterland. She trotted on and we could only just make out the top of the back of the calf now cantering behind, the sun on his back. She stopped again, and smelt, and looked, and listened, then she trotted on, getting smaller and smaller, and we could no longer hear her now, and we could not see the calf. Now we could just see her. Now we could not.

Then we went and made a camp in the shade of a big wide beautiful Lundi, and we slept.

Part Six

CHAPTER TWENTY-NINE

BACK in the Umfurudzi it was pretty hard, the earth hot, hard rocky stony deadgrass hot, and the river-beds hot heavy sand, and only the very largest water-holes had any water and the sun beat you down and beat off the earth and the hot blue horizon shimmered. It was the fag end of the Operation, at the end of September it would be too hot for man and beast, it was very nearly too hot for man now. The Umfurudzi was bad country now, there were only four rhinos left in that whole country, maybe six, but they were very far apart and they had become very wild. The first four long, hot, bad days Coetsee did not find any spoor at all. On the fifth day he and Kapesa found spoor of two beasts, and they tracked them and darted them. Sometimes it goes like that. For two more days they looked for spoor, but there was no spoor, the rhinos had all gone, or the poachers had got them. On the eighth day Coetsee moved his camp back to the Ruya to try to capture Thompson's last lone 'white' bull.

And the first hot dry morning Coetsee picked up the spoor of a lone large bull on the banks of the Ruya, the spoor was good and fresh, no more than a few hours old. Coetsee and Kapesa tracked him and got closer and closer, and it was very good that the last lone rhino of the Ruya would not live all alone. For four hours Coetsee tracked him and the spoor got very warm indeed and then Kapesa sighted him, three hundred yards off. And he was black, not white. And Coetsee darted him and he was black all right.

Then Paul Coetsee moved his camp four hundred miles, to the country called Tende Springs, near the Nyadowe river, up there north of Gokwe. It was the last move of the Operation, for that year. There were only two weeks to go. Coetsee took David Scammel with him in place of Old Norman. The colour of Scammel's hair is brown.

CHAPTER THIRTY

Now in the Tende there is much jesse, the thick tangled bush and heavy undergrowth, which is difficult and dangerous country. There are steep ravines and hills and many rocks. There are no elephants in the Tende and so there are no elephant paths through the dense tangled jesse, only the tunnels made by the rhinos, through which you have to creep. It is low-lying land, and very hot, and the wind changes constantly and you cannot see more than six feet ahead through the jesse. It is hard tracking country. You had to creep through the tunnels and duck under the entanglements and part the bush in front of you, crouch down to pick up the dead leaves from the place you wanted to put your foot, take one step, peer ahead, then lean on your knee again and clear the next place. Then one step again. Look. Listen. Test the wind. Then crouch again to clear the next place. And all the time with the wind changing. The Tende is very dangerous country in which to hunt a rhinoceros to kill him. It is almost suicidal country in which to try to catch him alive.

At sunrise on the second day Kapesa picked up the spoor at the water-hole in the Nyadowe. Coetsee had Scammel with the heavy calibre ·458 rifle. Young Nevin Lees-May stayed behind in camp to finish building the pens. The spoor was cold, several hours old. They tracked him north for three hours, and the wind was with them, but it was difficult tracking country. Then the spoor turned west across the Nyadowe, and then south, and then into very bad jesse. He was wandering, looking for a place to lie up. For one hour they tracked him through the hot dense jesse, one step at a time, and they had not seen him or heard or smelt him. Then the wind changed. The spoor indicated that the animal had become very agitated, he had smelt them. The killer beast was very close somewhere in there. Then they heard him. The big sudden angry snort and the big huffing and crash-ing. He charged away through the great jesse, furious and crashing, then across bad broken country, into the next stretch of jesse. They followed his spoor for half an hour through the jesse, then they heard him crashing out again. Then they saw him for the first time. He was five hundred yards away crashing uphill through the bad broken country, headed back into bad jesse. He was very angry and he knew he was being hunted.

The big bull went deep into the big jesse, a long way. Then he holed up. He did a semi-circle back on his tracks, then he holed up and waited for them.

Coetsee went in after him, alone. They had tracked him deep in, then Coetsee told Scammel and Kapesa to stop. He had heard the beast somewhere in there, just a snap of a twig. Co-etsee tested the wind, then he went in slowly through the thick jesse, making a semi-circle with the wind in towards the place he thought he had heard him. It was one o'clock, they had been tracking him for five hours. Coetsee could not see more than a few feet ahead. He went in very carefully and quietly with the wind in a semi-circle and he was concentrating all his will on the great murderous beast somewhere in there, but he could not dominate him until he saw him.

When he was three or four paces off from the beast Coetsee could smell him. He stopped dead still, senses racing, staring into the thick jesse, trying to see him, sense him, pin down where he was, the great killer beast he had to spring and dominate before it sprung and murdered him. For two minutes Coetsee stood dead-still like that, heart thudding, senses racing, listening for him in the great dense heat of the jesse, and the killer beast as tall as a man stood dead-still also, listening, sensing, smelling, red-eyed, murderous, furious, trying to see him to kill him; for two minutes they stood like that three or four paces apart, man and beast, and there was nothing in the world but their racing senses searching. And they could not sense each other precisely. Then Coetsee took one tense careful silent step, then another, and he saw the beast the moment it charged.

The rhinoceros that got Paul Coetsee crashed out of the jesse to his side, charged crashing roaring red-eyed at him from three paces off to kill him, smash its great horn right through his guts and spread them on the treetops; there was nothing in the world but the great sudden crash of the killer beast coming thundering out of nowhere to kill him, and Coetsee spun. Spun and leapt to his right in nerve-sprung instinctive reaction, the beast swiped its great neck at him, swiped past his guts by inches and thundered on. Coetsee reeled and raised his dart-gun to fire at the killer beast's rump and already the beast had spun on him. It spun in a yard and came crashing thundering straight back at Coetsee and he leapt aside and backwards through the jesse; the beast swiped at his guts and missed again, Coetsee leapt back and scrambled sideways, reeling, clutching, through the jesse and the beast crashed after him hooking, crashing, uprooting the thick jesse to get at Coetsee and kill him; Coetsee scrambled reeling, staggering, backwards, the jesse tore him open, he scrambled backwards crashing, clutching the dart-gun, zigzagging, bloody and the beast crashed after him roaring red-eyed uprooting the jesse to get at him and there was nothing in the world but their crashing, the beast one pace after him hooking at his guts to throw him through the air and kill him; for ten yards they crashed through the jesse so thick a man cannot see six feet ahead of him, then the beast got him. Hit him at full killer thunderous charge in the thigh and down to the bone and there was nothing in the shocked crashing world but the great crash of the murderous head and the sharp stink of it, and it hooked its great neck and flung him. Flung him cart-wheeling bloody up through the jesse, and the killer beast charged snorting prehistoric after him and as he came crashing bloody down through the jesse the beast swiped him again. Hit him through the thigh again with all its two-thousand-pound might before he hit the ground, and threw him again, cart-wheeling, through the jesse, and he came crashing back down on to the raging killer head again, and it swiped him again. Flung him back up through the jesse and he came crashing bloody down on to the beast's rump. Coetsee landed spread-eagled across the killer beast's rump. The beast looked around wildly, confused, for the man, to kill him. Then it lumbered backwards, snorting, trampling, into the jesse, still carrying Coetsee. Then it charged forward and threw him off its back.

The beast thundered to a halt. Coetsee crashed down on to his buttocks four feet behind the massive hind-legs. He was still clutching the dart-gun. The beast stood, wild-eyed, furious, great flanks heaving, confused; Coetsee sat there, stock-still, pumping blood, four feet behind it. One move, one sound and the killer beast would have spun on him. Torn, shocked, bloody, staring at it, willing it, will power racing – *you will not kill me.* For five long seconds they were like that, the motionless bloody man and the heaving, wild-eyed, killer beast, then it snorted and dropped its head. It crashed off through the jesse, crashing snorting, huffing, furious, and it was gone.

Coetsee dropped the gun. He tried to climb to his feet and the blood rushed out of his trousers. He clutched his thigh with both hands tight to close the biggest wound.

'*Kapesa!*' he shouted.

CHAPTER THIRTY-ONE

IT was one-thirty in the afternoon. There was no water. Coetsee lay on his side in the bloody jesse, tanned face white,
sweat running off him, hair matted, sweat running down his
legs into his big wounds. They were all sweating, shiny, Scammel binding him up feverishly, Kapesa, shocked, shining,
sweaty black, holding him, the sharp stink of the sweating
porters, staring *ah! ah!* Blood everywhere, his shorts black with
sticky blood, blood running down his legs, blood shining black
on the green jesse, blood shining red-black high in the branches,
the ground underneath him was muddy black with blood.
Scammel's hands were red with blood binding him.

'I thought you'd darted him and you were up a tree,' Scammel said.

Scammel pressed the special pad hard on to the gaping
wound. It had been made long ago by Coetsee's wife for just
this purpose. It was sodden with blood, Scammel bound it
tight. Coetsee lay propped on his elbow, ashen white, sweating,
directing him; Kapesa supported his shoulders.

'The other pads are too big for the other holes,' Scammel
sweated. He was ashen too, red hands shaking, he had never
done this before.

'Stuff cotton-wool in,' Coetsee said. 'Deep.'

Scammel plucked a big wad of cotton-wool off. Coetsee
screwed up his eyes. Scammel put the big wad over the big
bloody hole and took a breath and clenched his teeth and then
sunk his fingers into the hole. Kapesa held Coetsee tight, shining black. Scammel was ashen. He grabbed off another wad of
cotton-wool and clenched his teeth and rammed it into the
other hole and he was fumbling, ashen, sweating, bloody, for

the bandages and wrapping them feverishly tight around the leg. Then he snapped off the tip of the syringe of morphine and rammed it into Coetsee's good leg and pumped it into him. Then he shouted for Roger-Roger and tried to call up young Nevin at the base camp. For five minutes he worked, sweating, cursing on the radio, and the bloody thing was out of order. Then he left Coetsee lying with Kapesa and set off running flat out back to base camp.

There was no water. They had hunted this country in the old days together, Coetsee and Kapesa, and they knew the nearest water at this time of the year was at the base camp, on the Nyadowe river, twelve miles away. At first they talked a little, while the morphine worked, while Coetsee was a little euphoric under the drug. At first, with the morphine, it had seemed like some kind of bad joke to Coetsee, that the old soothsayer had been right and he had been wrong. Well the beast had not killed him, he had been right about that, no rhinoceros would kill Paul Coetsee, a lion maybe, an elephant maybe, more likely a poacher maybe, but not a rhinoceros. Then after an hour the morphine had worn off and the bad pain came back, and the thirst, dry mouth, dry throat rasping, sweating, waxen, and the ringing in his ears.

They heard the Land-Rover from a long way and it took a long time. The pain and the thirst was very bad now. At five o'clock Coetsee had his first drink of water. They loaded him on the Land-Rover and set off jolting, grinding through the bush to the airstrip called Tchoda. It took them one hour to do the ten miles over that country to Tchoda, going flat out. The Rhodesian Air Force light aircraft was waiting in the hot red sunset. They loaded Coetsee on to the stretcher, into the aircraft. At ten minutes past six it took off and wheeled over the hot sunset bush for Salisbury. At seven o'clock, half-way to Salisbury, the engine started misfiring.

CHAPTER THIRTY-TWO

THE moon had just risen. The small aeroplane was shuddering and misfiring harder and harder, losing power and altitude. Coetsee lay strapped to the stretcher; he twisted his head but he could not see what was happening, nor hear what the pilot was saying into the radio, he could only hear the misfires and the shuddering. His leg was bleeding badly again. He could feel the aircraft dropping, nose coming down, he shouted, but it was downed in the spluttering roaring. By the moonlight the pilot could make out a dirt road winding through the black bush way down there. The aircraft was losing altitude hard, the pilot was talking rapidly into the radio, giving his position. The pilot brought the plane roaring, spluttering, jolting, misfiring, down out of the black starlit African sky in the moonlight, down over the black night bush, spluttering, roaring, jolting, misfiring, and Coetsee felt his head go down and his legs come up and the hot rush of blood flooding and the throb in his leg. The pilot worked the controls and headed her for the rough silver strip of dirt road down there carved through the rushing black, he swung her lurching, backfiring, down and now the blackness was rushing, roaring, spluttering below the shaking wings and the blood was rushing to Coetsee's sickened head; the pilot swung the plane down and the black bush was rushing underneath his swinging wings now, ahead the silver road was shortening to a bend, he forced her nose down hard and the treetops were screaming past his wingtips, and the bend in the road was juddering rushing up, he pushed her down as hard as he dared and the big black trees at the bend were screaming at him faster faster, rushing, lurching faster closer, and it was no good. He wrenched back the joystick and the engines misfired and the nose lurched up on its momentum, wrenched her up as hard as he could and the treetops roared at them, big black closer closer closer, and then roaring underneath the wings. The aircraft spluttered up over the treetops, and beyond was a ploughed maize field. The plane came spluttering, juddering, misfiring, down over the black field, the wheels hit the rough ground and she jolted, went thundering, misfiring, jolting over the black field, and the nose wheel smashed into a ridge. Smashed the wheel and the nose crashed down, and the tail flew up, and Coetsee's stretcher tore loose from its mountings and smashed up against the fuselage. Smashed Coetsee's head against the fuselage, gashed open his eye, fractured his cheekbone, smashed him and the stretcher about the plane and there was nothing in the world but the crashing smashing. Then it was dead quiet. The plane stood on its nose in the African moonlight.

The pilot and the medical orderly got him out. At eight o'clock the Rhodesian Air Force helicopter found them. At nine o'clock they got Coetsee into Salisbury General Hospital. There was blood everywhere. On the rhino's horn. In the jesse. In the Land-Rover. In the aircraft. In the maize field. In the heli-copter. In the ambulance. The pain was very bad indeed.

CHAPTER THIRTY-THREE

THAT was the end of Operation Rhino for that year 1970. There were only thirteen days left to go, anyway, before it was scheduled to end. It was getting too hot, anyway, for man and beast. Next month the big rains would come.

Next year the Operation would start again. In the autumn, after the rains. Coetsee and Thompson would go back next year and get the three or four left in the Umfurudzi, and Coetsee's big bull in the Tende. If the poachers hadn't got them first. And the sixty or so other isolated rhinos left here and there, somewhere far away out there, before the poachers got them. Coetsee would be better again by then. There is plenty of room for them in the Gona-re-Zhou. There used to be many there fifty years ago. There used to be hundreds and hundreds of thousands, all over Africa, fifty years ago.

Well, at the time of writing there are forty-one rhinos in the Gona-re-Zhou. In fact Operation Rhino captured forty-three, but there was the pregnant cow which fell over the cliff, aborted and died, and then there was the cow, with the calf, who got snared, down into the bone: well, she recovered from the operation and they kept her in a stockade behind Osborne's house while she convalesced, and she did well, but the shock of the operation to remove the snare, or something, made her stop lactating. The calf, which was only six weeks old, sucked and sucked and sucked, but there was no milk, and he got thinner and thinner and weaker and weaker, in a few days, and he was too small to eat anything else. The cow with the bandage round her foreleg fretted about him, and she would not let anybody into the stockade to investigate, and when they grew alarmed at the calf's condition and shot a dose of M99 into the cow so they could get into the stockade, it was too late. They took him away from her and tried to feed him by bottle, and John Condy came down from Salisbury, but it was too late, and he died.

But, forty-one rhinos in the Gona-re-Zhou. And suppose Thompson and Coetsee get the other sixty that are out there, say there'll be one hundred rhinos in the Gona-re-Zhou. Say, an average natural increase, with a gestation period of seventeen or eighteen months, of between five to eight per cent per annum. That means that in say thirteen to fifteen years there will be two hundred rhinos in the Gona-re-Zhou. In thirty years, maybe four hundred. In fifty years? All right, in fifty years maybe there will be eight hundred rhinos in the Gona-re-Zhou, all things being equal.

But, you figure it out. What is the world going to be like in fifty years? Say in twenty-five years. The present world population, the Naked Ape population, despite two World Wars, Hitler and Hiroshima, Korea, the Congo, Vietnam, the Pill, and all the fashionable political purges, despite all the motor-car and airline crashes and multiple murders, is doubling itself about every twenty years. At the moment of writing there are three thousand five hundred million people in the world. There are nearly eight hundred million Chinese, one quarter of Mankind. Five hundred and fifty million Indians. Three hundred and fifty million Africans. Ten or twelve years ago, there were only two hundred odd million Africans.

Now, not counting the pollution, the atmosphere poisoned by industrial smoke which will, scientists say, shroud the earth from the vital rays of the sun, not counting the polluted seas and all the marine life poisoned from industrial waste, not counting the land denuded of the vegetation which, with the sun, makes the oxygen we breathe, so there will be not enough oxygen – not even counting all those killers, where will Africa be in twenty, forty, fifty years? In twenty years there will be three hundred rhinos in the Gona-re-Zhou, all things being equal; but all things will not be equal: in twenty years there will not be only three hundred and fifty million Africans in Africa but six or seven hundred million Africans, looking to the land.

You figure it out. What are the chances of anything? Something must be done. Anyway, next year Operation Rhino will go out again. To try.

POSTSCRIPT

THE next year, 1971, Operation Rhino resumed, from May to September, in the Kariba District, in dangerous country which is very broken with many streams with steep banks, rugged gorges and ravines. It is very difficult to get the recovery vehicles through such country. There is much bad jesse. There are also many elephant and buffalo there, which makes tracking and hunting extremely difficult. The jesse gives the rhino very good cover to hole up in.

Altogether they got thirty-eight rhino that year. But one female fell over a cliff after being darted, and died. Another female was badly injured, and had to be destroyed, when the translocation vehicle was involved in an accident. Two males died after capture, as result of bad bullet wounds previously inflicted by poachers.

The poaching in the Kariba District was found to be very bad. Skeletons of eight dead rhino were found. A number of the rhinos captured still had broken cable snares round their necks, some deeply embedded, festering; many others had old snare scars.

The last rhino in the 1971 Operation was the same beast that gored Coetsee the year before, in the Tende. For five days Coetsee and Kapesa and Scammel tracked him again.

The first day Coetsee found signs indicating that the beast had been wounded by poachers. He found pus scraped on to a branch, and there was a slight drag mark on the spoor, indicating that he had been wounded in the shoulder. That first day they made contact once. He charged through thick jesse before Coetsee could get a dart in. Coetsee dodged behind a tree, then up it, and the beast crashed and slashed the trunk murderously, then charged off.

The next three days they hunted him continuously, through thick jesse. He was covering great distances, he knew he was being hunted. And the poacher's wound had made him more savage. Coetsee went very, very carefully indeed. Several times his hunter's instinct told him to hold back: each time thereafter he found the place, right there, where the beast had been waiting to ambush him.

On the fifth day, the last day of Operation Rhino for that year, they picked up the spoor and followed it into very thick jesse. It was remarkable coincidence that the Operation was to end with the same beast, and the same man, as last year's. They followed the spoor for two hours. Suddenly Coetsee came upon him. He was fifteen paces away, and he was asleep. Coetsee was astonished.

He stalked to within six paces of the great beast that had savagely gored him last year, to get a clear shot, and the wind stayed right. Coetsee fired and the dart smacked home. And the great beast did not turn and charge savagely at him, it turned and fled.

They tracked him, and twenty minutes later they found him, unconscious. There was the big festering poacher's bullet wound, just behind the shoulder. As Coetsee went up to him, he took a big groaning breath, and died.

Paul Coetsee performed a post mortem operation. He opened up the festering poachers wound and found a shattered .303 soft-nosed bullet had glanced off the shoulder blade, chipped the first rib and severed the top of the lung. The wound was four weeks' old. The beast had died from renewed internal haemorrhage from this wound brought on by strain under the M99 drug.

That was the end of Operation Rhino for that year.

THE END

A SELECTION OF FINE READING AVAILABLE IN CORGI BOOKS

General

All these books are available at your bookshop or newsagent: or can be ordered direct from the publisher. Just tick the titles you want and fill in the form below.

CORGI BOOKS: Cash Sales Department, P.O. Box 11, Falmouth, Cornwall.
Please send cheque or postal order, no currency, and allow 7p per book to cover the cost of postage and packing in the U.K. (5p if more than one copy) 7p per book overseas.

NAME ....

ADDRESS ....

(OCTOBER 73) ....